Poems Comic and Serious

THOMAS HOOD
POEMS COMIC AND SERIOUS
Illustrated With His Humorous Woodcuts

Selected with an introduction and notes by
Peter Thorogood

The Bramber Press 1995

For
Roger

in affectionate memory
of his parents
Renée and Lawrence

The Bramber Press

First published in 1995 by
The Bramber Press
St. Mary's House,
Bramber, West Sussex, BN44 3WE
Tel: 01903 816205

ISBN 0 9526786 0 8

Original typesetting & graphics by Tony Ketteman

Printed in Great Britain by
smallprint
35 Silver Birches, Haywards Heath, West Sussex RH16 3PD

Preface

Thomas Hood was a poet of an unusual order of brilliance and invention. He was skilled in almost every form of poetic writing, being equally at home with romantic sonnets and love poems, poignant social poems like *The Song of the Shirt*, and *The Bridge of Sighs*, as well as with punning ballads such as *Faithless Sally Brown,* witty parodies and epigrams, sentimental songs and comic ditties for the music hall. He was also skilled in the creation of brilliantly sustained narrative satires and highly original humorous monologues.

The curse of a fragile constitution may, in part, account for the remarkable mental energy he summoned up to carry out his varied tasks, whether as sub-editor of *The London Magazine* or as editor of his own popular *Comic Annuals*. As a young man, he played the flute, he drew and sketched, he painted charming water colours and studied etching and engraving on copper and wood. His early poetry grew out of an admiration for Byron and Keats, yet he succeeded in creating both romantic and comic styles all his own. Even though poverty and illness pressed hard upon him, he developed an extraordinary talent for the comic in both his verse and his woodcuts. Furthermore, Hood's intense, "serious" humour aptly expresses a compassion for the underprivileged and oppressed part of human kind.

Day to day events were a constant source of inspiration for Hood: items of news, incidents and accidents, the famous and the infamous, among countless observations of daily life, moved in a great panorama before his keen editorial eye, providing him with a vast catalogue of details which he could draw on at will from his remarkably retentive memory. His need for new subjects was insatiable. Ideas filled his imagination with innumerable fancies which poured forth from an eager pen. As he wrote in one of his prefaces: *"In this motley world the most solemn events sometimes give birth to very comical issues."* His system of "Practical Philosophy" allows him to laugh heartily at the "Grotesques and Arabesques and droll Picturesques" that diverted him from the more sombre realities.

For many readers today, Thomas Hood's poetry and prose may seem to be like an "Old Curiosity Shop", crammed with unfamiliar bric-a-brac. On closer examination, we discover, among those dusty shelves and long-forgotten corners, riches of lasting value. Beneath the veil of contemporary reference and perilous punning lies a body of work that is worthy of a more respected place in our literature. Hood's daughter, Frances Freeling

Broderip, wrote in the Preface to her edition of her father's works: *"He wrote such pure, intelligible English. He speaks in his works to the great mass of the people in a tongue they can understand and thoroughly feel."*

Admired by Dickens, Thackeray and Edgar Allan Poe, Thomas Hood's work continued to influence writers over the next century: Christina Rossetti, Gerard Manley Hopkins, Baudelaire, T. S. Eliot, Sir John Betjeman and Philip Larkin, all owe, in some measure, a debt to Hood's genius – a testimony to Hood's continuing influence.

This selection of the shorter poems, together with some of the many woodcuts, commemorates the 150th anniversary of Thomas Hood's death. I have sought to make a choice from the shorter poems which reflects the variety of Hood's work, both comic and serious. For those readers who would like to explore the less familiar references in the poems and go beyond the visual pleasures and delights of the woodcuts, I have provided explanatory notes.

Peter Thorogood
St. Mary's, Bramber
October 1995

Acknowledgements

I would especially like to thank Robin Myers for her encouragement and generosity, without which this book could not have been published in its present form. I am also grateful to Tony Ketteman for his invaluable editorial assistance and to Roger Linton for his constant support over recent years in my Thomas Hood research.

Hood's design for his coat-of-arms

Contents

Political Poems

Social Protest

Epigrams

End Piece

*

The Woodcuts

*

A Circulating Library

INTRODUCTION

THOMAS HOOD
1799-1845

1. The Child and Schoolboy

Thomas Hood was born in London, within the sound of Bow Bells, on 23rd May 1799. A 'blue plaque' on the wall of what was once the site of number 31 The Poultry, now commemorates the event. His father had come south from Dundee to join the London publisher, Vernor, whose partner he was to become in due course. When Thomas was still a child, the family moved out to Islington, then a tranquil rural village on the outskirts of the City. He was described by one of his father's friends as a 'singular child, silent and retired, with much quiet humours and apparently delicate in health.'

In spite of his Scottish ancestry, Hood was always proud to be a Londoner:

> *Next to being a citizen of the world, it must be the best thing to be born a citizen of the world's greatest city ... a literary man should exult rather than otherwise that he first saw the light – or perhaps the fog – in the same metropolis as Milton, Gray, De Foe, Pope, Byron, Lamb and other town-born authors ...*

From an early age Hood enjoyed playing practical jokes. He had a special ability for turning sadness into laughter. The only person he ever frightened with a practical joke was himself, when, as a boy, he traced a diabolical face on the ceiling of the passage outside his bedroom, to frighten his brother as he came to bed. Forgetting his joke, and coming to bed early by mistake, he was so terrified by the phantom of his own making that he fled down the stairs in his nightshirt and burst into the drawing-room, crowded with his father's guests. Forty years later, his childish fears were immortalised in a fine descriptive poem entitled *The Haunted House:*

> *Such omens in the place there seemed to be,*
> *At every crooked turn, or on the landing,*
> *The straining eyeball was prepared to see*
> *Some Apparition standing.*
>
> *For over all there hung a cloud of fear,*
> *A sense of mystery the spirit daunted,*
> *And said, as plain as whisper in the ear,*
> *The place is Haunted!*

Hood's early education was gained at a Dame School, where he learnt little more than the three R's. From there, he proceeded to Dr. Wanostrocht's Academy for Young Gentlemen, and, echoing Gray's *Ode on a Distant Prospect of Eton College,* he composed his own version: *Ode on a Distant Prospect of Clapham Academy!*

> *Ah me! those old familiar bounds!*
> *That classic house, those classic grounds*
> *My pensive thought recalls!*
> *What tender urchins now confine,*
> *What little captives now repine*
> *Within yon irksome walls!*

2. The Artist and Engraver

The young Thomas spent much of his time in drawing and sketching, encouraged by his uncle, Robert Sands, the engraver of the popular series of illustrations of well-known London buildings. In *The Progress of Art*, Hood takes a wistful look back to his first art lessons when he abandoned crayon and chalk for the more adventurous Indian ink and water-colour:

> *Oh then, what black Mont Blancs arose,*
> *Crested with soot, and not with snows;*
> *What clouds of dingy hue!*
> *In spite of what the Bard has penned,*
> *I fear the distance did not "lend*
> *Enchantment to the view."*
>
> *But colours came! – like morning light,*
> *With gorgeous hues displacing night,*
> *Or Spring's enlivened scene;*
> *At once the sable shades withdrew;*
> *My skies got very, very blue;*
> *My trees extremely green.*

About 1814, following the death of his father, Hood joined a shipping firm in the City, but suffered a breakdown in health which forced him to renounce his mercantile career for that of engraving. A brief spell in the quiet of the Berkshire Downs, under the tutelage of his uncle, Robert, resulted in a series of charming water colours. He was later apprenticed to the prestigious

Le Keux brothers for whom he produced some excellent etchings for their topographical publications. Once more his health broke with a severe attack of fever, the effects of which were to remain with him for the rest of his life. By way of recuperation, he was sent to stay with his aunt in Dundee, where he remained for two years. There he was able to enjoy, in his own words, "the contemplative quiet, the sweet wholesome air, and the picturesque scenery". Life in the town inspired the precocious fifteen-year old to compose an amusing account of it in rhyming couplets, *Dundee Guide*, much in the style of Anstey's *New Bath Guide*. Fortified by the Scottish air, Hood returned to London in 1817 and at once applied for apprenticeship as an engraver and etcher.

3. The Sub-Editor

On the death of his mother in 1821, Hood, now twenty two years of age, was left to bring up his four sisters. He wrote to his old friend, George Rollo, in Dundee: "I have suffered an inexpressible anguish of mind in parting from my only parent, and but for the consolations I have had, I should have sunk under it". Few poets have recorded more poignantly such anguish and grief at bereavement as expressed by Hood in his poem *The Death-Bed*:

> *Our very hopes belied our fears,*
> *Our fears our hopes belied –*
> *We thought her dying when she slept,*
> *And sleeping when she died.*

By 1818, the literary publication, *The London Magazine*, was at the height of its popularity, numbering among its contributors, Charles Lamb, William Hazlitt, Thomas De Quincey, and the young Thomas Hood.

On the night of 16th February 1821, a duel took place at Chalk Farm between John Scott, editor of the *London*, and Jonathan Christie, friend of John Gibson Lockhart, editor of *Blackwood's Magazine*. Scott had vehemently attacked Lockhart and the resulting bitterness between the two men grew out of all proportion. Scott was mortally wounded, though he lingered for another eleven days. A friend of Hood's father came to the rescue, bought up the *London*, eventually offering Hood a sub-editorship, by way of supplementing the family income. In his *Literary Reminiscences*, Hood has left us some enduring portraits of his contemporaries: John Clare "shining verdantly out of the grave-coloured suits of the literati in his bright grass-coloured coat, and yellow waistcoat", Coleridge, whose fine flowing voice carried the young poet "spiralling up to heaven by a whirlwind intertwisted with sunbeams" and Charles Lamb, who was to become one of Hood's greatest friends, "a figure remarkable at a glance, with a fine head on a small spare body, supported by two almost immaterial legs".

Such was the splendid circle of friends in which Hood found himself. He was on the threshold of a new career as poet and humorist. Only one thing stood in his way – his wish to be accepted as a serious poet.

4. The Romantic Poet

One of Hood's greatest friends on the staff of the *London* was the fanciful and whimsical poet, John Hamilton Reynolds, who introduced him to the poetry of John Keats, a strong influence on Hood's romantic verse. Hood soon became a regular visitor to the Reynolds household at Little Britain, close by St. Bartholomew's, where he met Reynolds' lively sisters, Marianne, Charlotte, and Jane, the last of whom had been the recipient of the letter from Keats announcing that he had "thrown Endymion into the sea". It appears Mrs Reynolds had other plans for her daughter, Jane, and opposed any idea of marriage to a poorly paid sub-editor with pretensions to becoming a "comic" poet! However, Thomas and Jane succeeded in announcing their engagement in the autumn of 1822 and Hood wrote his prospective mother-in-law a long conciliatory letter. Hood shows a spontaneous warmth and affection in his letters to the family into which he was to marry.

In 1824, Hood had a relapse and spent some time convalescing at Islington. On 5th May Thomas and Jane were married at St. Botolph's Church, Aldersgate, and left for their honeymoon at Hastings. Hood now began to capitalise on his publishing experience, employing his skills as engraver as well as comic poet. Byron had provided the stimulus, both social and political, for Hood's first book, *Odes and Addresses to Great People*, the frontispiece of which was a clever etching entitled *The Progress of Cant*, one of the most elaborate of processional caricatures. Keats, however, was the first major influence on Hood's serious Romantic verse, much of which at this time was assembled in a volume entitled *The Plea of the Midsummer Fairies, Hero and Leander, Lycus the Centaur, and Other Poems*. Whilst the longer title poems have their fine moments, it is the shorter poems which have taken their place in the anthologies on our library shelves: *Fair Ines,* odes to *Autumn* and *Melancholy, The Sea of Death,* and well-turned sonnets, *To Fancy* and *Silence.*

One of the best known poems in this volume is *Ruth:*

> *She stood breast high amid the corn,*
> *Clasp'd by the golden light of morn,*
> *Like the sweetheart of the sun,*
> *Who many a glowing kiss had won.*

5. The Comic Poet

Thomas and Jane moved into rooms in Robert Street, Adelphi. By now, all the great Romantic poets, except Wordsworth, had died. Of the minor poets in Hood's day – Felicia Hemans, George Darley, and the mysterious L.E.L. (Letitia Elizabeth Landon), none was substantial enough to fill the literary void. Hood could not hope to satisfy his public in his serious vein. They wanted not tears but laughter, and he accordingly published his two phenomenally successful volumes of *Whims and Oddities*. Through Charles and Mary Lamb the Hoods came to know the popular actress, Fanny Kelly, for whom Hood wrote a number of comic, punning ballads. From this time on, his prodigious talent for punning was to remain his hallmark. Public taste demanded it and few but Hood could provide the hungry reader with such tasty morsels.

> *Oh Thomas Hood! Thou soul of fun,*
> *I know not one in London*
> *Better than thee to make a pun,*
> *Or better to be punn'd on!*

His punning ballads *Faithless Sally Brown, Tim Turpin, Mary's Ghost, Lieutenant Luff, Sally Simpkin's Lament,* and *Faithless Nelly Gray,* established Hood as the leading comic writer of his day. Hood's range of comic writing is considerable: the gentle irony of the *Parental Ode to My Son* and *Domestic Asides, or Truth in Parenthesis,* boldly facetious poems like *Faithless Sally Brown,* comic effects in the triple end-rhymes of *A Nocturnal Sketch*, the comic long lines of *Our Village* (cleverly imitated by Ogden Nash) and brilliantly sustained rhymes of *Ode to Rae Wilson,* and *Miss Kilmansegg and Her Precious Leg* – all these poems and many more show Hood to possess a phenomenal range of linguistic and poetic skills unequalled by any of his immediate contemporaries.

In the closing months of 1827, Hood suffered a severe attack of rheumatic fever and was ordered to Brighton to convalesce. There, he could enjoy the company of his father's old friends, the brilliant and witty authors of *Rejected Addresses*, Horace and James Smith. Hood's lifelong battle with illness frequently frustrated his publishing projects and left him too much weakened to write, though he had his occasional outbursts of defiance:

> *I'm sick of gruel, and the dietetics,*
> *I'm sick of pills, and sicker of emetics,*
> *I'm sick of pulses' tardiness and quickness,*
> *I'm sick of blood, its thinness and its thickness, –*
> *In short, within a word, I'm sick of sickness!*

6. The Story Teller

In 1828, Hood, undeterred by ill-health, embarked on yet another venture. Keats had given Jane the manuscript of his poem *On a Picture of Leander*. This she offered to Hood for what was to be a new Annual, entitled *The Gem*. Contributions came from Charles Lamb, John Clare, Thomas Moore, and Sir Walter Scott. The book was an astounding success with all 5,000 copies of the first edition sold. In spite of its glittering array of talent, by far the most sensational and compelling contribution was by Hood himself. *The Dream of Eugene Aram* was to bring Hood fame and fortune and a more sophisticated readership, both at home and abroad. The poem is a powerful example of Hood's skill in writing narrative verse and its impact on the reading public was phenomenal. Aram, a schoolmaster at Lynn, had murdered a shoemaker for his gold. Years later, after the unearthing of a skeleton, Aram was arrested, and in a sensational trial, made an eloquent though unsuccessful defence. He was hanged in 1759. Hood takes the moment when the murderer, in an effort to relieve his tormented soul, confesses his crime to an innocent child in his care:

> *All night I lay in agony,*
> *From weary chime to chime,*
> *With one besetting horrid hint,*
> *That rack'd me all the time, –*
> *A mighty yearning like the first*
> *Fierce impulse unto crime!*

> *One stern tyrannic thought, that made*
> *All other thoughts its slave;*
> *Stronger and stronger every pulse*
> *Did that temptation crave, –*
> *Still urging me to go and see*
> *The Dead Man in his grave!*

Hood now moved into a happier period of his life, enjoying the company of many new friends and ever-increasing popularity and success. Possibly with a view to being closer to the Lambs, or because of a desire for a more rural setting and healthier country air, he and Jane moved to Enfield, where they had discovered a delightful house, Rose Cottage, on Winchmore Hill, with a sheltered garden filled with trees and flowering shrubs. He acquired a generous patron, the Duke of Devonshire, and embarked upon a series of *Comic Annuals* – a popular admixture of humorous poems and stories, with some fifty woodcuts engraved from his own designs.

The dedication of the *Comic Annual* for 1832 to William IV led to the King's wish to meet England's most famous comic poet. In spite of his frail condition, Hood set out on the seven-hour journey to Brighton. On arrival at the Royal Pavilion, he was received in a cordial and hearty manner. All went well until, on retiring, he backed out of the royal presence and forgot where the door was; the King good-naturedly laughed and showed his serio-comic guest the way out, going with him as far as the door.

Hood, flushed with success, decided to move house again, partly through a disagreement with his landlord at Rose Cottage and partly through *folie de grandeur*. In the extravagant surroundings of Lake House, at Wanstead in Essex, he could entertain his friends in the grand style. The house, with its fading murals, classical portico and its lake, was set in acres of land. This move he was very much to regret. In spite of a deep sense of loss at the death of his old friend Charles Lamb, Hood soldiered on through a series of wrangles with his publishers (there were few copyright laws to speak of in his day), and battling all the time with a serious, consumptive condition. When attacks of fever grew worse, he was compelled to work from his bed, suffering alarming attacks of breathlessness and intermittent bouts of blood-spitting. Not to be defeated, he launched into the fight, in company with Dickens, to reform the copyright laws.

7. The Exile

1835 was a year in which Hood experienced a flurry of misfortunes that would all but crush his spirit. The birth of their son, Tom, brought Jane to the very edge of death. Gravely ill, she had to be nursed by her ailing husband in conditions little short of poverty. The Reynolds now berated Hood for his extravagance and he broke with them. His generosity in entertaining friends in style further hastened his financial collapse. Threatened with destitution and mounting debts, he had no alternative but to leave England. Rather than face the degradation of the Debtors' Prison, he courageously bade an emotional farewell to his wife and children, in the most distressing of circumstances, and set sail for Rotterdam. A great storm rose up off the coast of Holland. The steam ship was buffeted violently by gigantic waves, its passengers and crew believing their very lives to be in peril. Hood's physical condition was aggravated almost beyond endurance and he landed at Rotterdam in a state of utter physical exhaustion.

From Rotterdam, he proceeded alone to Coblenz, where he took furnished rooms in the Castor Hof, just below the confluence of the Rhine and Moselle. The difficulties and inconveniences of publishing his works from such a distance can only be imagined. Eventually, Jane and the children were able to join him. They found him terribly emaciated by his sufferings, though bravely full of spirit and hope, still playing his practical jokes – he tried to persuade Jane not to buy plaice with red spots because it was not fresh! It was typical of Hood that his uncomfortable German exile should result in a comical account of his travels entitled *Up the Rhine*.

8. The Social Poet

The years of suffering spent abroad to clear his debts brought Hood close to the suffering of others, especially the dire predicament of the London poor. His whole life now was taken up with causes – his relentless fight against cant and hypocrisy, his determination to take to task any public figure or situation – and composing, for example, powerful diatribes like *Ode to Sir Andrew Agnew* and *Ode to Rae Wilson,* on the Lord's Day Observance Bill.

Incredibly, despite the increasing weakness of not only liver, but also heart and lungs, Hood completed work on one of his most brilliant verse narratives: *Miss Kilmansegg and Her Precious Leg: A Golden Legend,* concerning the pedigree, birth, christening, childhood, education, courtship, marriage and subsequent murder of the fabulously rich Miss Kilmansegg, whose whole existence was suffused with the glint and glimmer of gold. As a commentary on the acquisition of wealth for its own sake, the poem is one of the most brilliantly sustained satires of the Victorian period. The description of Miss Kilmansegg's parents shows how deftly Hood could evoke his subject through the virtuosity of his language and imagery:

> *To paint the maternal Kilmansegg*
> *The pen of an Eastern Poet would beg,*
>   *And need an elaborate sonnet;*
> *How she sparkled with gems whenever she stirred,*
> *And her head niddle-noddled at every word,*
> *And seemed so happy, a Paradise Bird*
>   *Had nidificated upon it.*
>
> *And Sir Jacob the Father strutted and bowed,*
> *And smiled to himself, and laughed aloud*
>   *To think of his heiress and daughter –*
> *And then in his pockets he made a grope,*
> *And then, in the fullness of joy and hope*
> *Seemed washing his hands in invisible soap*
>   *In imperceptible water.*

Following a riding accident, Miss Kilmansegg loses a leg, and chooses an artificial one of solid gold. At a ball, she meets a spurious foreign Count, falls in love and marries him. Ominously, her honeymoon is described in images of silver rather than of gold, for her dastardly husband will murder her on her wedding night by hitting her over the head with her own leg. At his trial he is acquitted on the grounds that, since she was killed by her own leg, it was obviously a case of suicide!

9. The Uncrowned Laureate

The appearance of the Christmas number of *Punch* on the 16th December 1843 assured Hood of a permanent place in the annals of socio-political verse. In the previous October, a seamstress named Biddle, was charged at Lambeth Police Court with pawning articles belonging to her employer. She was a poor widow with several children to feed and clothe. During the interrogation she revealed that she was able to earn only seven shillings a week and that her employer considered this a perfectly good living wage.

The case provoked indignation in all sections of society. *The Times* published a strongly-worded leader on the incident, and *Punch* took up the cudgels in an article entitled "Famine and Fashion". Hood, inspired by such abject poverty, sat down and wrote his poem at a single sitting. He showed it to Jane. As it was being wrapped up, she remarked: "Now mind, Hood, mark my words, this will tell wonderfully! It is one of the best things you ever did!"

> *With fingers weary and worn,*
> *With eyelids heavy and red,*
> *A Woman sat, in unwomanly rags*
> *Plying her needle and thread –*
> *Stitch! stitch! stitch!*
> *In poverty, hunger, and dirt,*
> *And still with a voice of dolorous pitch*
> *She sang the "Song of the Shirt!"*

The Song of the Shirt became the most talked-about poem of the year. It trebled the circulation of *Punch*, was reprinted in *The Times*, as well as in countless other newspapers and journals. It was printed on scarves; it was printed on handkerchiefs; it was sung in the streets by the poor to a tune of their own. The poem became overnight something of a folk song, touching the heart and conscience of the nation.

In March 1843, the Poet Laureate, Robert Southey, died. The post of Laureate fell vacant. Neither Robert Browning nor Tennyson had published their major work. Among the best known of the minor poetic voices of the day were Mrs. Felicia Hemans, Letitia Elizabeth Landon, Thomas Beddoes, and the "Corn Law" poet, Ebenezer Elliott. There is no doubt that Hood towered above these in the breadth of his work because of his genius for comic verse, for tender, nostalgic poems, and his popular appeal through his volumes of *Whims and Oddities* and *Comic Annuals*. The ageing Wordsworth, the only poet of any real stature at that time, lived on in retirement, busily watering down the passionate poetry of his youth to suit Victorian taste. To his many admirers, Hood seemed a likely candidate for the laureateship, but a "comic" author was not thought to possess sufficient dignity for the post of Court Poet. Had he lived in the age of Betjeman (a great admirer), Hood undoubtedly would have been chosen for the position. Eventually Wordsworth was appointed, though it cannot be said that he added in any way to the poetic stature of Laureate. We wonder with what poetic *tours de force*, with what sublime comicalities, Hood would have entertained his adoring readers. He would certainly have been delighted with his public role and no doubt he would have poured forth a torrent of memorable verbal pyrotechnics to prove it.

10. The Compassionate Poet

In spite of sickness, Hood took on the editorship of the *New Monthly Magazine*, but the publisher, Colburn, resented Hood's new-found fame. The work, too, was demanding and unremunerative. Hood resigned, only to take on a further challenge in the publication of yet another of his long-wished-for projects: *Hood's Monthly Magazine and Comic Miscellany*, which flourished under his able editing. Although distinguished contributors included Charles Dickens, Sir Edward Bulwer Lytton and Robert Browning, Hood was able, once more, to out-shine them all with his powerful, evocative poem, *The Haunted House*.

Charles Cowden Clarke, meeting Hood at a friend's house in 1844, wrote that his *"worn, pallid look strangely belied the effect of jocularity and high spirits conveyed in his writings. He punned incessantly, but languidly, almost as if unable to think in any other way than in play on words. His smile was attractively sweet; it bespoke the affectionately-hearted man which his serious verses – those especially addressed to his wife or his to his children – show him to be, and it also showed the depth of pathos in his soul that inspired* Song of the Shirt, Eugene Aram, Bridge of Sighs*"*.

Abject poverty was never more than a stone's throw away from the London streets "paved with gold". The case of Mary Furley, who, in desperation, threw herself from Westminster Bridge, clutching her newly-born child in her arms, caused public outcry when she was sentenced to death for murder and attempted suicide. The plight of this destitute mother and child drew from Hood's pen one of his most admired poems, *The Bridge of Sighs*:

> *One more Unfortunate,*
> *Weary of breath,*
> *Rashly importunate,*
> *Gone to her death!*
>
> *Take her up tenderly,*
> *Lift her with care:*
> *Fashion'd so slenderly,*
> *Young and so fair!*

Hood's faith in human nature was again to be severely tested. False dealings by printers and publishers once more brought on one of his attacks of breathlessness. His family doctor arranged a birthday party for him but he was too sick to attend. Still, he defiantly penned more verses: *The Lay of the Labourer, The Workhouse Clock* and *The Lady's Dream*, in all of which he drew from his readers feelings of both compassion and indignation.

11. The Last Days

Pleased as he was at such a sensational response to his poems, Hood was frequently irritated by the futility of political controversy, especially when it clouded the effect of his humanitarian message. His purely political utterances are few, frank, and brief:

> *For my part, I say, hang party! there wants a true country party to look singly to the good of England – retrench and economise, reduce taxes, and make it possible to live as cheap at home as abroad. There would be patriotism, instead of mere struggle of Ins and Outs for place and pelf.*

The Prime Minister, Sir Robert Peel, out of admiration for Hood's work, conferred on Jane a life pension. Hood wrote to Thackeray: "King Death will claim me ere many months elapse. However, there's a good time coming. If not in this world, most assuredly in the next". Thackeray, in his turn reminisced:

> *What he has to do he does with all his might, through sickness, through sorrow, through exile, poverty, fever, depression, there he is, always ready to work, with a jewel of genius in his pocket. When he laid down his puns and pranks, put the motley off, and spoke out of his heart, all England and America listened with tears and wonder ... Oh, sad, marvellous picture of courage, of honesty, of patient endurance, of duty struggling against pain.*

Hood now had little time in this world, but he was not going to leave it without a quip or two:

> *I seem to have retained my shadow and sold my substance. In short, as happens with prematurely old port wine, I am of a bad colour with very little body ... I have converted a serious illness into a comic wellness – by what other agency could I have transported myself, as a Cockney would*

say, from Dullage to Grinage. It was far from a practical joke to be laid up in a foreign land, under the care of Physicians, quite as much abroad as myself with the case ... but I resolved, that like the sun, so long as my day lasted, I would look at the bright side of everything. The raven croaked, but I persuaded myself that it was the nightingale: There was the smell of the mould, but I remembered that it nourished the violets.

Hood lay looking out of his window at the newness of nature as it flowered and flourished.

It is a beautiful world since I have been lying here. I have thought of it more and more; it is not so bad, even humanly speaking, as people make it out. I have had some happy days while I lived in it, and I could have wished to stay a little longer in it. But it is all for the best, and we shall meet in a better world.

Soon after this, he fell into a delirium. Thirty-six hours later, his family at his bedside, he passed into that happier world he had so much hoped for. It was mid-day on the 3rd May 1845, just three weeks before his forty sixth birthday. As Jane could not afford to pay the costs of his interment in the Poets Corner at Westminster Abbey, he was buried in Kensal Green Cemetery, beside many famous contemporaries. For several years the grave remained without a headstone, but, on 18th July 1854, his monument was at last unveiled by one of his distinguished admirers, Richard Monckton Milnes (later Lord Houghton). Standing nearby, among his many friends, were humble men and women who had come to honour their poet, and to read the simple epitaph:

"He sang the Song of the Shirt"

Hood's design for his tombstone

ROMANTIC
POEMS

I REMEMBER, I REMEMBER

I remember, I remember,
The house where I was born,
The little window where the sun
Came peeping in at morn;
He never came a wink too soon
Nor brought too long a day,
But now, I often wish the night
Had borne my breath away!

I remember, I remember,
The roses, red and white,
The violets, and the lily-cups,
Those flowers made of light!
The lilacs where the robin built,
And where my brother set
The laburnum on his birthday, –
The tree is living yet!

I remember, I remember,
Where I was used to swing,
And thought the air must rush as fresh
To swallows on the wing;
My spirit flew in feathers then,
That is so heavy now,
And summer pools could hardly cool
The fever on my brow!

I remember, I remember,
The fir trees dark and high;
I used to think their slender tops
Were close against the sky:
It was a childish ignorance,
But now 'tis little joy
To know I'm further off from heav'n
Than when I was a boy.

The Lady of "Our Village"

Fly Fishing

FAIR INES

O saw ye not fair Ines?
She's gone into the West,
To dazzle when the sun is down,
And rob the world of rest:
She took our daylight with her,
The smiles that we love best,
With morning blushes on her cheek,
And pearls upon her breast.

O turn again, fair Ines,
Before the fall of night,
For fear the Moon should shine alone,
And stars unrivall'd bright;
And blessed will the lover be
That walks beneath their light,
And breathes the love against thy cheek
I dare not even write!

Would I had been, fair Ines,
That gallant cavalier,
Who rode so gaily by thy side,
And whisper'd thee so near! –
Were there no bonny dames at home
Or no true lovers here,
That he should cross the seas to win
The dearest of the dear?

I saw thee, lovely Ines,
Descend along the shore,
With bands of noble gentlemen,
And banners wav'd before;
And gentle youth and maidens gay,
And snowy plumes they wore; –
It would have been a beauteous dream,
– If it had been no more!

Alas, alas, fair Ines,
She went away with song,
With Music waiting on her steps,
And shoutings of the throng;
But some were sad, and felt no mirth,
But only Music's wrong,
In sounds that sang Farewell, Farewell,
To her you've loved so long.

Farewell, farewell, fair Ines,
That vessel never bore
So fair a lady on its deck,
Nor danc'd so light before, –
Alas for pleasure on the sea,
And sorrow on the shore!
The smile that blest one lover's heart
Has broken many more!

SONG:
FOR MUSIC

A lake and a fairy boat
To sail in the moonlight clear, –
And merrily we would float
From the dragons that watch us here!

Thy gown should be snow-white silk,
And strings of orient pearls,
Like gossamers dipp'd in milk,
Should twine with thy raven curls!

Red rubies should deck thy hands,
And diamonds should be thy dow'r –
But Fairies have broke their wands,
And wishing has lost its pow'r!

AUTUMN

The Autumn skies are flush'd with gold,
And fair and bright the rivers run;
These are but streams of winter cold,
And painted mists that quench the sun.

In secret boughs no sweet birds sing;
In secret boughs no bird can shroud;
These are but leaves that take to wing,
And wintry winds that pipe so loud.

'Tis not trees' shade, but cloudy glooms
That on the cheerless vallies fall,
The flowers are in their grassy tombs,
And tears of dew are on them all.

BALLAD

It was not in the winter
    Our loving lot was cast!
It was the time of roses
    We plucked them as we passed!

That churlish season never frowned
    On early lovers yet! –
Oh no – the world was newly crowned
    With flowers, when first we met.

'Twas twilight, and I bade you go,
    But still you held me fast; –
It was the time of roses, –
    We plucked them as we passed!

What else could peer my glowing cheek
    That tears began to stud? –
And when I asked the like of Love
    You snatched a damask bud, –

And oped it to the dainty core
    Still glowing to the last: –
It was the time of roses,
    We plucked them as we passed!

TO - - -

Welcome, dear Heart, and a most kind good-morrow;
The day is gloomy, but our looks shall shine: –
Flow'rs I have none to give thee, but I borrow
Their sweetness in a verse to speak for thine.

Here are red roses, gather'd at thy cheeks, –
The white were all too happy to look white:
For love the rose, for faith the lily speaks;
It withers in false hands, but here 'tis bright!

Dost love sweet Hyacinth? Its scented leaf
Curls manifold, – all love's delights blow double:
'Tis said this flow'ret is inscribed with grief, –
But let that hint of a forgotten trouble.

I pluck'd the Primrose at night's dewy noon;
Like Hope, it show'd its blossoms in the night; –
'Twas, like Endymion, watching for the Moon!
And here are Sun-flowers, amorous of light!

These golden Buttercups are April's seal, –
The Daisy stars her constellations be:
These grew so lowly, I was forced to kneel,
Therefore I pluck no Daisies but for thee!

Here's Daisies for the morn, Primrose for gloom,
Pansies and Roses for the noontide hours: –
A wight once made a dial of their blooms, –
So may thy life be measur'd out by flow'rs!

SONG

There is dew for the flow'ret
    And honey for the bee,
And bowers for the wild bird,
    And love for you and me.

There are tears for the many
    And pleasures for the few;
But let the world pass on, dear,
    There's love for me and you.

RUTH

She stood breast high amid the corn,
Clasp'd by the golden light of morn,
Like the sweetheart of the sun,
Who many a glowing kiss had won.

On her cheek an autumn flush,
Deeply ripened; – such a blush
In the midst of brown was born,
Like red poppies grown with corn.

Round her eyes her tresses fell,
Which were blackest none could tell,
But long lashes veil'd a light,
That had else been all too bright.

And her hat, with shady brim,
Made her tressy forehead dim; –
Thus she stood amid the stooks,
Praising God with sweetest looks: –

Sure, I said, heav'n did not mean,
Where I reap thou shouldst but glean,
Lay thy sheaf adown and come,
Share my harvest and my home.

SONNET: TO FANCY

Most delicate Ariel! submissive thing,
Won by the mind's high magic to its hest, –
Invisible embassy, or secret guest, –
Weighing the light air on a lighter wing: –
Whether into the midnight moon to bring
Illuminate visions to the eye of rest, –
Or rich romances from the florid West. –
Or to the sea, for mystic whispering, –
Still by thy charm'd allegiance to the will,
The fruitful wishes prosper in the brain.
As by the fingering of fairy skill, –
Moonlight, and waters, and soft music's strain,
Odours, and blooms, and *my* Miranda's smile,
Making this dull world an enchanted isle.

SONNET

Love, dearest Lady, such as I would speak
Lives not within the humour of the eye; –
Not being but an outward phantasy,
That skims the surface of a tinted cheek, –
Else it would wane with beauty, and grow weak,
As if the rose made summer, – and so lie
Amongst the perishable things that die,
Unlike the love which I would give and seek:
Whose health is of no hue – to feel decay
With cheeks' decay, that have a rosy prime.
Love is its own great loveliness alway,
And takes new lustre from the touch of time;
Its bough owns no December and no May,
But bears its blossom into Winter's clime.

THE EXILE

The swallow with summer
   Will wing o'er the seas,
The wind that I sigh to
   Will visit thy trees,
The ship that it hastens
   Thy ports will contain,
But me – I must never
   See England again!

There's many that weep there
   But one weeps alone,
For the tears that are falling
   So far from her own;
So far from thy own, love,
   We know not our pain;
If death is between us,
   Or only the main.

When the white cloud reclines
   On the verge of the sea,
I fancy the white cliffs,
   And dream upon thee;
But the cloud spreads its wings
   To the blue heav'n and flies.
We never shall meet, love,
   Except in the skies!

Hook and Eye

SONG

The stars are with the voyager
    Wherever he may sail;
The moon is constant to her time;
    The sun will never fail;
But follow, follow round the world,
    The green earth and the sea;
So love is with the lover's heart,
    Wherever he may be.

Wherever he may be, the stars
    Must daily lose their light;
The moon will veil her in the shade;
    The sun will set at night.
The sun may set, but constant love
    Will shine when he's away;
So that dull night is never night,
    And day is brighter day.

The Jack of Hearts

BALLAD

Spring it is cheery,
　Winter is dreary
Green leaves hang, but the brown must fly;
　When he's forsaken,
　Wither'd and shaken
What can an old man do but die?

　Love will not clip him,
　Maids will not lip him,
Maud and Marian pass him by;
　Youth it is sunny,
　Age has no honey, –
What can an old man do but die?

　June it was jolly,
　O for its folly!
A dancing leg and a laughing eye;
　Youth may be silly,
　Wisdom is chilly, –
What can an old man do but die?

　Friends they are scanty,
　Beggars are plenty,
If he has followers, I know why;
　Gold's in his clutches,
　(Buying him crutches!)
What can an old man do but die?

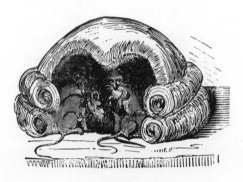

Wigwam

SERENADE

Ah, sweet, thou little knowest how
   I wake and passionate watches keep;
And yet while I address thee now,
   Methinks thou smilest in thy sleep.
'Tis sweet enough to make me weep,
   That tender thought of love and thee,
That while the world is hush'd so deep,
   Thy soul's perhaps awake to me!

Sleep on, sleep on, sweet bride of sleep!
   With golden visions for thy dower,
While I this midnight vigil keep,
   And bless thee in thy silent bower;
To me 'tis sweeter than the power
   Of sleep, and fairy dreams unfurl'd,
That I alone, at this still hour,
   In patient love outwatch the world.

STANZAS

Is there a bitter pang for love removed,
   O God! The dead love doth not cost more tears
Than the alive, the loving, the beloved –
   Not yet, not yet beyond all hopes and fears!
      Would I were laid
      Under the shade
Of the calm grave, and the long grass of years, –

That love might die with sorrow: – I am sorrow;
   And she, that loves me tenderest, doth press
Most poison from my cruel lips, and borrow
   Only new anguish from the old caress;
      Oh, this world's grief
      Hath no relief
In being wrung from a great happiness.

Would I had never filled thine eyes with love,
   For love is only tears: would I had never
Breathed such a curse-like blessing as we prove;
   Now, if "Farewell" *could* bless thee, I would sever;
      Would I were laid
      Under the shade
Of the cold tomb, and the long grass for ever!

TO A FALSE FRIEND

Our hands have met, but not our hearts:
Our hands will never meet again.
Friends, if we have ever been,
Friends we cannot now remain:
I only know I loved you once,
I only know I loved in vain;
Our hands have met, but not our hearts;
Our hands will never meet again!

Then farewell to heart and hand!
I would our hands had never met:
Even the outward form of love
Must be resign'd with some regret.
Friends, we still might seem to be,
If I my wrong could e'er forget;
Our hands have join'd, but not our hearts;
I would our hands had never met!

THE DEATH BED

We watch'd her breathing thro' the night,
Her breathing soft and low,
As in her breast the wave of life
Kept heaving to and fro!

So silently we seemed to speak –
So slowly moved about!
As we had lent her half our powers
To eke her living out!

Our very hopes belied our fears
Our fears our hopes belied –
We thought her dying when she slept,
And sleeping when she died!

For when the morn came dim and sad –
And chill with early showers,
Her quiet eyelids closed – she had
Another morn than ours!

STANZAS

Farewell, Life! My senses swim;
And the world is growing dim;
Thronging shadows cloud the light,
Like the advent of the night, –
Colder, colder, colder still
Upwards steals a vapour chill –
Strong the earthy odour grows –
I smell the Mould above the Rose!

Welcome, Life! the Spirit strives!
Strength returns, and hope revives;
Cloudy fears and shapes forlorn
Fly like shadows at the morn, –
O'er the earth there comes a bloom –
Sunny light for sullen gloom,
Warm perfume for vapour cold –
I smell the Rose above the Mould!

A Winter Nosegay

HUMOROUS
POEMS

A PARENTAL ODE TO MY SON,
AGED THREE YEARS AND FIVE MONTHS

Thou happy, happy elf!
(But stop, – first let me kiss away that tear) –
Thou tiny image of myself!
(My love, he's poking peas into his ear!)
  Thou merry, laughing sprite!
  With spirits feather-light,
Untouch'd by sorrow and unsoil'd by sin –
(Good heavens! the child is swallowing a pin!)

Thou little tricksy Puck!
With antic toys so funnily bestuck,
Light as the singing bird that wings the air –
(The door! the door! he'll tumble down the stair!)
  Thou darling of thy sire!
(Why, Jane, he'll set his pinafore a-fire!)
  Thou imp of mirth and joy!
In love's dear chain so strong and bright a link,
Thou idol of thy parents – (Drat the boy!
  There goes my ink!)

Thou cherub – but of earth
Fit playfellow for Fays, by moonlight pale,
  In harmless sport and mirth,
(That dog will bite him if he pulls its tail!)
  Thou human humming-bee, extracting honey
From ev'ry blossom in the world that blows,
Singing in Youth's Elysium ever sunny –
(Another tumble – that's his precious nose!)

Thy father's pride and hope!
(He'll break the mirror with that skipping-rope!)
With pure heart newly stamp'd from Nature's mint –
(Where *did* he learn that squint?)
  Thou young domestic dove!
(He'll have that jug off, with another shove!)
  Dear nursling of the hymeneal nest!
  (Are those torn clothes his best!)
  Little epitome of man!
(He'll climb upon the table, that's his plan!)
Touch'd with the beauteous tints of dawning life –
  (He's got a knife!)

Thou enviable being!
No storms, no clouds, in thy sky foreseeing,
  Play on, play on,
  My elfin John!
Toss the light ball – bestride the stick –
(I knew so many cakes would make him sick!)
With fancies buoyant as the thistledown,
Prompting the face grotesque, and antic brisk,
  With many a lamb-like frisk –
(He's got the scissors, snipping at your gown!)

  Thou pretty opening rose!
(Go to your mother, child, and wipe your nose!)
Balmy, and breathing music like the South,
(He really brings my heart into my mouth!)
Fresh as the morn, and brilliant as its star, –
(I wish that window had an iron bar!)
Bold as the hawk, yet gentle as the dove –
  (I'll tell you what, my love,
I cannot write, unless he's sent above!)

Fancy Portrait – Mr Malthus

THE SWEETS OF YOUTH

Time was I liked a cheesecake well enough;
  All human children have a sweetish taste –
I used to revel in a pie, or puff,
  Or tart – we all were *tartars* in our youth;
To meet with jam or jelly was good luck,
  All candies most complacently I crumped,
A stick of liquorice was good to suck,
  And sugar was as often liked as lumped;
On treacle's "linked sweetness long drawn out,"
  Or honey, I could feast like any fly,
I thrilled when lollipops were hawk'd about,
  How pleased to compass hard bake or bull's eye,
How charmed if fortune in my power cast
  Elecampane – but that campaign is past!

*

SONNET

I had a Gig-Horse, and I called him Pleasure,
  Because, on Sundays, for a little jaunt,
He was so fast and showy, quite a treasure;
  Although he sometimes kicked and shied aslant.
I had a Chaise, and christen'd it Enjoyment,
  With yellow body, and the wheels of red,
Because 'twas only used for one employment,
  Namely, to go wherever Pleasure led.
I had a wife, her nickname was Delight;
  A son called Frolic, who was never still;
Alas! how often dark succeeds to bright!
  Delight was thrown, and Frolic had a spill,
Enjoyment was upset and shattered quite,
  And Pleasure fell a splitter on *Paine's Hill*!

Fancy Portrait – Madame Hengler

Rocket-time at Vauxhall – A Prominent Feature

SONNET TO VAUXHALL

The cold transparent ham is on my fork –
    It hardly rains – and hark the bell! – ding-dingle –
Away! Three thousand feet at gravel work,
    Mocking a Vauxhall shower! – Married and Single
Crush – rush; – Soak'd Silks with wet white Satin mingle.
    Hengler! Madame! round whom all bright sparks lurk,
Calls audibly on Mr and Mrs Pringle
    To study the Sublime, &c – (vide Burke)
All Noses are upturn'd! – Wish – ish! – On high
    The rocket rushes – trails – just steals in sight –
Then droops and melts in bubbles of blue light –
    And Darkness reigns – Then balls flare up and die –
Wheels whiz – smack crackers – serpents twist – and then
    Back to the cold transparent ham again!

*

SONNET

The sky is glowing in one ruddy sheet; –
A cry of fire! resounds from door to door;
And westward still the thronging people pour; –
The turncock hastens to F.P. 6 feet,
And quick unlocks the fountains of the street;
While rumbling engines, with increasing roar,
Thunder along to luckless Number Four,
Where Mr Dough makes bread for folks to eat.
And now through blazing frames, and fiery beams,
The Globe, the Sun, the Phoenix, and what not,
With gushing pipes throw up abundant streams,
On burning bricks, and twists, on rolls – too hot –
And scorching loaves, – as if there were no shorter
And cheaper way of making toast and water!

A NOCTURNAL SKETCH

Even is come; and from the dark Park, hark
The signal of the setting sun – one gun!
And six is sounding from the chime, prime time
To go and see the Drury Lane Dane slain, –
Or hear Othello's jealous doubt spout out, –
Or Macbeth raving at that shade-made blade,
Denying to his frantic clutch much touch; –
Or else to see Ducrow with wide stride ride
Four horses as no other man can span;
Or in the small Olympic Pit, sit split
Laughing at Liston, while you quiz his phiz.

Anon Night comes, and with her wings brings things
Such as, with his poetic tongue, Young sung;
The gas up-blazes with its bright white light,
And paralytic watchmen prowl, howl, growl,
About the streets and take up Pall-Mall Sal,
Who, hasting to her nightly jobs, robs fobs.

Now thieves to enter for your cash, smash, crash,
Past drowsy Charley in a deep sleep, creep.
But frightened by Policemen B.3, flee,
And while they're going, whisper low, "No go!"

Now puss, while folks are in their beds, treads leads,
And sleepers waking, grumble – "Drat that cat!"
Who in the gutter caterwauls, squalls, mauls
Some feline foe, and screams in shrill ill-will.

Now Bulls of Bashan, of a prize size, rise
In childish dreams, and with a roar gore poor
Georgy, or Charley, or Billy, willy-nilly; –
But Nursemaid in a nightmare rest, chest-press'd,
Dreameth of one of her old flames, James Games,
And that she hears – what faith is man's – Ann's banns
And his, from Reverend Mr Rice, twice, thrice:
White ribbons flourish, and a stout shout out,
That upward goes, shows Rose knows those bows' woes!

NO!

No sun – no moon!
No morn – no noon –
No dawn – no dusk – no proper time of day –
No sky – no earthly view –
No distance looking blue –
No road – no street – no "t'other side the way" –
No end to any Row –
No indications where the Crescents go –
No top to any steeple –
No recognitions of familiar people –
No courtesies for showing 'em –
No knowing 'em! –
No travelling at all – no locomotion,
No inkling of the way – no notion –
"No go" – by land or ocean –
No mail – no post –
No news from any foreign coast –
No Park – no Ring – no afternoon gentility –
No company – no nobility –
No warmth, no cheerfulness, no healthful ease,
No comfortable feel in any member –
No shade, no shine, no butterflies, no bees,
No fruits, no flowers, no leaves, no birds, –
November!

November
Engraved by John Leech

DOMESTIC ASIDES:
OR TRUTH IN PARENTHESES

"I really take it very kind,
This visit Mrs Skinner!
I have not seen you such an age –
(The wretch has come to dinner!)

"Your daughters, too, what loves of girls –
What heads for painters' easels!
Come here and kiss the infant, dears –
(And give it p'rhaps the measles!)

"Your charming boys I see are home
From Reverend Mr Russel's;
'Twas very kind to bring them both, –
(What boots for my new Brussels!)

"What! little Clara left at home?
Well now I call that shabby:
I should have lov'd to kiss her so, –
(A flabby, dabby, babby!)

"And Mr.S., I hope he's well,
Ah! though he lives so handy,
He never now drops in to sup, –
(The better for our brandy!)

"Come, take a seat – I long to hear
About Matilda's marriage;
You're come, of course, to spend the day! –
(Thank Heav'n, I hear the carriage!)

"What! must you go? next time I hope
You'll give me longer measure;
Nay – I shall see you down the stairs –
(With most uncommon pleasure!)

"Good-bye! good-bye! remember all
Next time you'll take your dinners!
(Now, David, mind I'm not at home
In future to the Skinners!)"

THE DOCTOR

There once was a Doctor,
(No foe to the proctor,)
A physic-concocter,
Whose dose was so pat,
However it acted
One speech it extracted, –
"Yes, yes," said the Doctor,
"I meant it for that!"

And first, all unaisy,
Like woman that's crazy
In flies Mistress Casey,
"Do come to poor Pat,
The blood's running faster!
He's torn off the plaster –
"Yes, yes," said the Doctor,
"I meant it for that!"

Anon, with an antic,
Quite strange and romantic,
A woman comes frantic –
"What could you be at?
My darling dear Aleck,
You've sent him oxalic!"
"Yes, yes," said the Doctor,
"I meant it for that!"

Then in comes another,
Despatch'd by his mother,
A blubbering brother,
Who gives a rat-tat –
"Oh, poor little sister
Has lick'd off a blister!"
"Yes, yes," said the Doctor,
"I meant it for that!"

Now home comes the flunkey,
His own powder-monkey,
But dull as a donkey –
With basket and that –
"The draught for the Squire, Sir,
He chuck'd in the fire, Sir – "
"Yes, yes," said the Doctor,
"I meant it for that!"

The next is the pompous
Head Beadle, old Bumpus –
"Lord! here is a rumpus:
That pauper, Old Nat,
In some drunken notion
Has drunk up his lotion –"
"Yes, yes," said the Doctor,
"I meant it for that !"

At last comes a servant,
In grief very fervent:
"Alas! Doctor Derwent,
Poor Master is flat!
He's drawn his last breath, Sir –
That dose was his death, Sir."
"Yes, yes," said the Doctor,
"I meant it for that!"

An Unfortunate Bee-ing

BAILEY BALLAD
Love With A Witness

He has shav'd off his whiskers and blacken'd his brows
Wears a patch and a wig of false hair, –
But it's him – Oh it's him! – we exchanged lover's vows
When I lived up in Cavendish Square.

He had beautiful eyes, and his lips were the same,
And his voice was as soft as a flute –
Like a Lord or a Marquis he look'd, when he came
To make love in his master's best suit.

If I lived for a thousand long years from my birth,
I shall never forget what he told;
How he lov'd me beyond the rich women of earth,
With their jewels and silver and gold!

When he kiss'd me, and bade me adieu with a sigh,
By the light of the sweetest of moons,
Oh how little I dreamt I was bidding good-bye
To my Missis's tea-pot and spoons!

Protecting the Fare

FAITHLESS SALLY BROWN

Young Ben he was a nice young man,
   A carpenter by trade;
And he fell in love with Sally Brown,
   That was a lady's maid.

But as they fetch'd a walk one day,
   They met a press-gang crew;
And Sally she did faint away,
   Whilst Ben he was brought to.

The Boatswain swore with wicked words,
   Enough to shock a saint,
That though she did seem in a fit,
   'Twas nothing but a feint.

"Come, girl," said he, "hold up your head,
   He'll be as good as me;
For when your swain is in our boat,
   A boatswain he will be."

So when they'd made their game of her,
   And taken off her elf,
She roused, and found she only was
   A coming to herself.

"And is he gone, and is he gone?"
   She cried and wept outright:
"Then I will to the water side,
   And see him out of sight."

A waterman came up to her, –
   "Now, young woman," said he
"If you weep on so, you will make
   Eye-water in the sea."

"Alas! they've taken my beau Ben
   To sail with old Benbow;"
And her woe began to run afresh,
   As if she'd said Gee woe!

Says he, "They've only taken him
  To the Tender ship, you see;"
"The Tender-ship," cried Sally Brown,
  "What a hard-ship that must be!"

"O! would I were a mermaid now,
  For then I'd follow him;
But Oh! – I'm not a fish-woman,
  And so I cannot swim."

"Alas! I was not born beneath
  The virgin and the scales,
So I must curse my cruel stars,
  And walk about in Wales."

Now Ben had sail'd to many a place
  That's underneath the world;
But in two years the ship came home,
  And all her sails were furl'd.

But when he call'd on Sally Brown,
  To see how she went on,
He found she'd got another Ben,
  Whose Christian-name was John.

"O Sally Brown, O Sally Brown,
  How could you serve me so?
I've met with many a breeze before,
  But never such a blow."

Then reading on his 'bacco box
  He heav'd a bitter sigh,
And then began to eye his pipe,
  And then to pipe his eye.

And then he tried to sing "All's Well,"
  But could not though he tried;
His head was turn'd, and so he chew'd
  His pigtail till he died.

His death, which happen'd in his berth,
  At forty-odd befell:
They went and told the sexton, and
  The sexton toll'd the bell.

CONVEYANCING

O, London is the place for all,
    In love with loco-motion!
Still to and fro the people go
    Like billows of the ocean;
Machine or man, or caravan,
    Can all be had for paying,
When great estates, or heavy weights,
    Or bodies want conveying.

There's always hacks about in packs,
    Wherein you may be shaken,
And Jarvis is not always *drunk,*
    Tho' always *overtaken*;
In racing tricks he'll never mix,
    His nags are in their last days,
And *slow* to go, altho' they show
    As if they had their *fast days*!

Then if you like a single horse,
    This age is quite a *cab-age,*
A car not quite so small and light
    As those of our Queen *Mab* age;
The horses have been *broken well,*
    All danger is rescinded,
For some have *broken both their knees,*
    And some are *broken winded.*

If you've a friend at Chelsea end,
    The stages are worth knowing –
There is a sort, we call 'em short,
    Although the longest going –
For some will stop at Hatchett's shop,
    Till you grow faint and sicky,
Perched up behind, at last to find,
    Your dinner is all *dickey*!

Long stages run from every yard:
    But if you're wise and frugal,
You'll never go with any Guard
    That plays upon a bugle,
'Ye banks and braes,' and other-lays
    And ditties everlasting,
Like miners going all your way,
    With *boring* and with *blasting*.

Instead of *journeys*, people now
    May go upon a *Gurney*,
With steam to do the horse's work,
    By *powers of attorney*;
Tho' with a load it may explode,
    And you may all be *un*-done!
And find you're going *up to Heav'n*,
    Instead of *Up to London*!

To speak of every kind of coach,
    It is not my intention;
But there is still one vehicle
    Deserves a little mention;
The world a sage has call'd a stage,
    With all its living lumber,
And Malthus swears it always bears
    Above the proper number.

The law will transfer house or land
    For ever and a day hence,
For lighter things, watch, brooches, rings,
    You'll never want conveyance;
Ho! stop the thief! my handkerchief!
    It is no sight for laughter –
Away it goes, and leaves my nose
    To join in running after!

The "Short Stage" – A Mile End Omnibus

A Legal Conveyance

SALLY SIMPKIN'S LAMENT

"Oh! what is that comes gliding in,
　　And quite in middling haste?
It is the picture of my Jones,
　　And painted to the waist.

"It is not painted to the life,
　　For where's the trowsers blue?
Oh Jones, my dear! – Oh dear! my Jones,
　　What is become of you?"

"Oh! Sally dear, it is too true, –
　　The half that you remark
Is come to say my other half
　　Is bit off by a shark!

"Oh! Sally, sharks do things by halves,
　　Yet most completely do!
A bite in one place seems enough,
　　But I've been bit in two.

"You know I once was all your own,
　　But now a shark must share!
But let that pass – for now to you
　　I'm neither here nor there.

"Alas! death has a strange divorce
　　Effected in the sea,
It has divided me from you,
　　And even me from me!

"Don't fear my ghost will walk o' nights
　　To haunt as people say;
My ghost can't walk, for, oh! my legs
　　Are many leagues away!

"Lord! think when I am swimming round
　　And looking where the boat is,
A shark just snaps away a *half*,
　　Without a *quarter's* notice.

"One half is here, the other half
　　Is near Columbia placed;
Oh! Sally, I have got the whole
　　Atlantic for my waist.

"But now, adieu – a long adieu!
　　I've solved death's awful riddle,
And would say more, but I am doomed
　　To break off in the middle."

Sea-Consumption – Waisting Away

YOUTH AND AGE

Impatient of his childhood,
　　"Ah me!" exclaims young Arthur,
Whilst roving in the wild wood,
　　"I wish I were my father!"
Meanwhile, to see his Arthur
　　So skip, and play, and run,
"Ah me! exclaims the father,
　　"I wish I were my son!"

POLITICAL
POEMS

VERSES MISTAKEN FOR AN INCENDIARY

Come, all conflagrating fellows,
Let us have a glorious rig:
Sing old Rose, and burn the bellows
Burn me, but I'll burn my wig!

Christmas time is all before us:
Burn all puddings, north and south.
Burn the Turkey – Burn the Devil!
Burn snap-dragon! burn your mouth.

Burn the coals! They're up at sixty!
Burn Burn's Justice – burn Old Coke.
Burn the chestnuts! Burn the shovel!
Burn a fire, and burn the smoke!

Burn burnt almonds. Burn burnt brandy.
Let all burnings have a turn.
Burn Chabert, the Salamander, –
Burn the man that wouldn't burn!

Burn the old year out, don't ring it;
Burn the one that must begin.
Burn Lang Syne; and, whilst you're burning,
Burn the burn he paidled in.

Burn the boxing! Burn the Beadle!
Burn the baker! Burn his man!
Burn the butcher – Burn the dustman,
Burn the sweeper if you can!

Burn the Postman! burn the postage,
Burn the knocker – burn the bell!
Burn the folks that come for money!
Burn the bills – and burn 'em well.

Burn the Parish! Burn the rating!
Burn all taxes in a mass.
Burn the Paving! Burn the Lighting
Burn the burners! Burn the gas!

Burn all candles, white or yellow –
Burn the war and not for peace;
Burn the Czar of all the Tallow!
Burn the King of all the Greece!

Burn all canters – burn in Smithfield.
Burn Tea-Total hum and bug.
Burn his kettle, burn his water,
Burn his muffin, burn his mug!

Burn the breeks of meddling vicars,
Picking holes in Anna's Urns!
Burn all Steer's Opodeldoc,
Just for being good for burns.

Burn all Swindlers! Burn Asphaltum!
Burn the money-lenders down –
Burn all schemes that burn one's fingers!
Burn the Cheapest House in town!

Burn all Boz's imitators!
Burn all tales without a head!
Burn a candle near the curtain!
Burn your Burns, and burn your bed!

Burn all wrongs that won't be righted,
Burn poor Soup, and Spanish claims –
Burn that Bell, and burn his Vixen!
Burn all sorts of burning shames!

Burn the Whigs! and burn the Tories!
Burn all parties, great and small!
Burn that everlasting Poynder –
Burn his Suttees once for all!

Burn the fop that burns tobacco.
Burn a Critic that condemns. –
Burn Lucifer and all his matches!
Burn the fool that burns the Thames!

Burn all burning agitators –
Burn all torch-parading elves!
And oh! burn Parson Stephen's speeches,
If they haven't burnt themselves.

STANZAS

With the good of our country before us,
　　Why play the mere partisan's game?
Lo! the broad flag of England is o'er us,
　　And behold on both sides 'tis the same!

Not for this, not for that, not for any,
　　Not for these, not for those, but for all, –
To the last drop of blood, – the last penny –
　　Together let's stand, or let's fall!

Tear down the vile signs of a fraction,
　　Be the national banner unfurl'd
And if we must have any faction, –
　　Be it 'Britain against all the world.'

Seeing a Review

SOCIAL
PROTEST

THE LADY'S DREAM

The lady lay in her bed,
  Her couch so warm and soft,
But her sleep was restless and broken still;
  For turning oft and oft
From side to side, she mutter'd and moan'd
  And toss'd her arms aloft.

At last she startled up,
  And gaz'd on the vacant air,
With a look of awe, as if she saw
  Some dreadful phantom there –
And then in the pillow she buried her face
  From visions ill to bear.

The very curtain shook,
  Her terror was so extreme;
And the light that fell on the broider'd quilt
  Kept a tremulous gleam;
And her voice was hollow, and shook as she cried: –
  'Oh me! that awful dream!

'That weary, weary walk
  In the churchyard's dismal ground!
And those horrible things, with shady wings,
  That came and flitted round, –
Death, death, and nothing but death,
  In every sight and sound!

'And oh! those maidens young,
  Who wrought in that dreary room,
With figures drooping and spectres thin,
  And cheeks without a bloom; –
And the Voice that cried, "For the pomp of pride,
  We haste to an early tomb!

' "For the pomp and pleasure of Pride,
  We toil like Afric slaves,
And only to earn a home at last,
  Where yonder cypress waves;" –
And then they pointed – I never saw
  A ground so full of graves!

'And still the coffins came,
    With their sorrowful trains and slow;
Coffin after coffin still,
    A sad and sickening show;
From grief exempt I never had dreamt
    To such a World of Woe!

'Of the hearts that daily break,
    Of the tears that hourly fall,
O the many, many troubles of life,
    That grieve this earthly ball –
Disease and Hunger, and Pain, and Want,
    But now I dreamt of them all!

'For the blind and the cripple were there,
    And the babe that pined for bread,
And the houseless man, and the widow poor
    Who begged – to bury the dead;
The naked, alas, that I might have clad,
    The famished I might have fed!

'The sorrow I might have soothed,
    And the unregarded tears;
For many a thronging shape was there,
    From long forgotten years.
Ay, even the poor rejected Moor,
    Who rais'd my childish fears!

'Each pleading look, that long ago
    I scann'd with a heedless eye,
Each face was gazing as plainly there,
    As when I pass'd it by:
Woe, woe for me if the past should be
    Thus present when I die!

'No need of sulphurous lake,
    No need of fiery coal,
But only that crowd of human kind
    Who wanted pity and dole –
In everlasting retrospect –
    Will wring my sinful soul!

'Alas! I have walked through life
  Too heedless where I trod;
Nay, helping to trample my fellow worm,
  And fill the burial sod –
Forgetting that even the sparrow falls
  Not unmark'd of God!

'I drank the richest draughts;
  And ate whatever is good –
Fish, and flesh, and fowl, and fruit,
  Supplied my hungry mood;
But I never remembered the wretched ones
  That starve for want of food!

'I dress'd as the noble dress,
  In cloth of silver and gold,
With silk, satin, and costly furs,
  In many an ample fold;
But I never remembered the naked limb
  That froze with winter's cold.

'The wounds I might have heal'd!
  The human sorrow and smart!
And yet it never was in my soul
  To play so ill a part:
But evil is wrought by want of Thought,
  As well as want of Heart!'

She clasp'd her fervent hands,
  And the tears began to stream;
Large, and bitter, and fast they fell,
  Remorse was so extreme:
And yet, oh yet, that many a Dame
  Would dream the Lady's Dream!

Dream

THE SONG OF THE SHIRT

With fingers weary and worn,
  With eyelids heavy and red,
A Woman sat, in unwomanly rags,
  Plying her needle and thread –
    Stitch! stitch! stitch!
In poverty, hunger, and dirt,
And still with a voice of dolorous pitch
She sang the "Song of the shirt!"

  'Work! work! work!
While the cock is crowing aloof!
  And work – work – work,
Till the stars shine through the roof!
It's O! to be a slave
  Along with the barbarous Turk,
Where woman has never a soul to save,
  If this is Christian work!

  'Work – work – work
Till the brain begins to swim;
  Work – work – work
Till the eyes are heavy and dim!
Seam, and gusset, and band,
  Band, and gusset, and seam,
Till over the buttons I fall asleep,
  And sew them on in a dream!

'O! Men with Sisters dear!
  O! Men with Mothers and Wives!
It is not linen you're wearing out,
  But human creatures' lives!
    Stitch – stitch – stitch,
  In poverty, hunger, and dirt,
Sewing at once with a double thread,
  A Shroud as well as a Shirt.

'But why do I talk of Death?
  That Phantom of grisly bone,
I hardly fear his terrible shape,
  It seems so like my own –
  It seems so like my own –,
  Because of the fasts I keep,
Oh! God! that bread should be so dear,
  And flesh and blood so cheap!

'Work – work – work!
  My labour never flags;
And what are its wages? A bed of straw,
  A crust of bread – and rags.
That shatter'd roof, – and this naked floor –
  A table – a broken chair –
And a wall so blank, my shadow I thank
  For sometimes falling there!

  'Work – work – work!
From weary chime to chime,
  Work – work – work –
As prisoners work for crime!
  Band, and gusset, and seam,
  Seam, and gusset, and band,
Till the heart is sick, and the brain benumb'd,
  As well as the weary hand.

'Work – work – work!
In the dull December light,
  And work – work – work,
When the weather is warm and bright –
While underneath the eaves
  The brooding swallows cling
As if to show me their sunny backs
  And twit me with the spring.

  'Oh! but to breathe the breath
Of the cowslip and primrose sweet –
  With the sky above my head,
And grass beneath my feet,
For only one short hour
  To feel as I used to feel,
Before I knew the woes of want
  And the walk that costs a meal!

'Oh! but for one short hour!
  A respite however brief!
No blessed leisure of Love or Hope,
  But only time for Grief!
A little weeping would ease my heart,
  But in their briny bed
My tears must stop, for every drop
  Hinders needle and thread!'

Seam, and gusset, and band,
Band, and gusset, and seam,
     Work, work, work,
Like the Engine that works by Steam!
A mere machine of iron and wood
     That toils for Mammon's sake –
Without a brain to ponder and craze
     Or a heart to feel – and break!

With fingers weary and worn,
     With eyelids heavy and red,
A Woman sat in unwomanly rags,
     Plying her needle and thread –
          Stitch! stitch! stitch!
     In poverty, hunger and dirt,
And still with a voice of dolorous pitch,
Would that its tone could reach the Rich! –
     She sang this "Song of the Shirt!"

A "Constable's Miscellany"

THE BRIDGE OF SIGHS

One more Unfortunate,
Weary of breath,
Rashly importunate,
Gone to her death!

Take her up tenderly,
Lift her with care;
Fashion'd so slenderly,
Young, and so fair!

Look at her garments
Clinging like cerements;
Whilst the wave constantly
Drips from her clothing;
Take her up instantly,
Loving, not loathing. –

Touch her not scornfully;
Think of her mournfully,
Gently and humanly;
Not of the stains of her,
All that remains of her
Now is pure womanly.

Make no deep scrutiny
Into her mutiny
Rash and undutiful:
Past all dishonour
Death has left on her
Only the beautiful.

Still, for all slips of hers,
One of Eve's family –
Wipe those poor lips of hers
Oozing so clammily.

Loop up her tresses
Escaped from the comb,
Her fair auburn tresses;
Whilst wonderment guesses
Where was her home?

Who was her father?
Who was her mother?
Had she a sister?
Had she a brother?
Or was there a dearer one
Still, and a nearer one
Yet, than all other?

Alas! for the rarity
Of Christian charity
Under the sun!
Oh! it was pitiful!
Near a whole city full,
Home she had none!

Sisterly, brotherly,
Fatherly, motherly,
Feelings had changed:
Love, by harsh evidence,
Thrown from its eminence;
Even God's providence
Seeming estranged.

Where the lamps quiver
So far in the river;
With many a light
From window and casement,
From garret to basement,
She stood, with amazement,
Houseless by night.

The bleak wind of March
Made her tremble and shiver;
But not the dark arch,
Or black flowing river:
Mad from life's history,
Glad to death's mystery
Swift to be hurl'd –
Anywhere, anywhere,
Out of the world!

In she plunged boldly,
No matter how coldly
The rough river ran, –
Over the brink of it,
Picture it – think of it,
Dissolute man!
Lave in it, drink of it,
Then, if you can!

Take her up tenderly,
Lift her with care;
Fashion'd so slenderly,
Young, and so fair!

Ere her limbs frigidly
Stiffen too rigidly,
Decently, – kindly, –
Smoothe and compose them;
And her eyes, close them,
Staring so blindly!

Dreadfully staring
Thro' muddy impurity,
As when with the daring
Last look of despairing,
Fix'd on futurity.

Perishing gloomily,
Spurr'd by contumely,
Cold inhumanity,
Burning insanity,
Into her rest. –
Cross her hands humbly,
As if praying dumbly,
Over her breast!

Owning her weakness,
Her evil behaviour,
And leaving with meekness,
Her sins to her Saviour!

EPIGRAMS

THE SUPERIORITY OF MACHINERY

A Mechanic his labour will often discard
 If the rate of his pay he dislikes;
But a clock – and its *case* is uncommonly hard –
Will continue to work though it *strikes*.

*

A REFLECTION

When Eve upon the first of Men
 The apple press'd with specious cant
Oh what a thousand pities then
 That Adam was not Adamant!

*

ON THE ARRANGEMENT OF THE STATUES
IN TRAFALGAR SQUARE

If Nelson looks down on a couple of Kings,
 However it pleases the Loyals;
'Tis after the fashion of nautical things,
 A Sky-scraper over the Royals.

*

ON A CERTAIN EQUESTRIAN STATUE

Whoever has looked upon Wellington's breast,
Knows well that he is not so full in the chest;
But the sculptor, to humour the Londoner's partial,
Has turn'd the lean Duke to a plump City Marshall.

An Anti-Climax

A Non-Sequitur

PARTY SPIRIT

"Why did you not dine," said a Lord to a Wit,
  "With the Whigs, you political sinner?"
"Why really I meant, but had doubts how the *Pit*
  Of my stomach would bear a Fox dinner."

*

ON LIEUTENANT EYRE'S NARRATIVE
OF THE DISASTERS OF CABUL

A sorry tale of sorry plans,
Which this conclusion grants,
That Afghan clans had all the *Khans*
And we had all the can'ts.

*

EPIGRAM

My heart's wound up just like a watch,
  As far as springs will take –
It wants but one more evil turn,
  And then the cords will break!

*

ON THE DEATH OF A GIRAFFE

They say, God Wot!
She died upon the spot:
But then in spots she was so rich, –
I wonder which!

END PIECE

TO MINERVA
From the Greek

My temples throb, my pulses boil,
   I'm sick of Song and Ode, and Ballad –
So Thrysis, take the Midnight Oil –
   And pour it on a lobster salad.

My Brain is dull, my sight is foul,
   I cannot write a verse, or read –
Then, Pallas, take away thine Owl,
   And let us have a lark instead.

A Highland Fling

NOTES TO
THE POEMS

p.31 *I Remember, I Remember. (Friendship's Offering 1826 / Plea of the Midsummer Fairies 1827).* Hood wrote to his boyhood friend, George Rollo, in Dundee on 7th February 1820: *"... when seen from the valley, the summit of the mountain appears to touch the skies; but when we have ascended and reached its top, we seem, and no doubt are, as far from heaven as ever!"* In this poem Hood is more likely to be remembering the family's new home in Islington rather than his birth place in The Poultry.

p.33 *Fair Ines. (London Magazine 1823 / Plea 1827).*

p.34 *Song: For Music. (Plea 1827).*

p.34 *Autumn. (Plea 1827).*

p.35 *Ballad: It was not in the winter. (Literary Souvenir 1827).*

p.35 *To - - -: Welcome, dear heart. (Plea 1827). v.6 wight* = creature.

p.36 *Song: There is dew for the flow'ret.*

p.36 *Ruth. (Forget-me-not 1827 / Plea 1827).* In the *Ode to a Nightingale* Keats has the lines:

> *The voice I hear this passing night was heard*
> *In ancient days by emperor and clown:*
> *Perhaps the self-same song that found a path*
> *Through the sad heart of Ruth, when, sick from home,*
> *She stood in tears amid the alien corn.*

Although *Ruth* has echoes of Wordsworth's *Solitary Reaper*, Hood turns, like Keats, to the original story of the girl who toils in a far-off land, a gleaner in the fields of Boaz. On seeing her amid the corn, Boaz asks how she came there. Impressed by her gentle and generous nature, he eventually takes her as his wife. The 'hymnal' stanza is reminiscent of a harvest thanksgiving. The Dean of Canterbury Cathedral, Henry Alford (1810-1871), later echoed Hood's image and seven-syllable line in the concluding couplet of his well-known harvest hymn:

> *Come, with all Thine Angels come;*
> *Bid us sing Thy Harvest-home.*

p.37 *Sonnet: To Fancy. (London Magazine 1822 / Plea 1827).* Here,

Shakespeare's *The Tempest* has inspired one of the most beautiful of Hood's sonnets. l.2 *hest* = behest (command).

p.37 *Sonnet: Love, dearest Lady. (Plea 1827).*

p.38 *The Exile. (Plea 1827).*

p.39 *Song: The stars are with the voyager. (Plea 1827).*

p.40 *Ballad: Spring it is cheery. (Plea 1827).* cf. Robert Burns: "What can a Young Lassie do wi' an Auld Man."

p.42 *The Death Bed. (Englishman's Magazine 1831).* These lines are said to have been written on the death of Hood's sister, Anne. Hood's son, Tom, however, believed the poem was written as early as 1825 and it is just possible that the poem may have been inspired by the death of Hood's mother. The description of the horror of doubt as he looks at the dying patient in the dread stillness of the sickroom influenced Sir John Betjeman in the writing of his poem *Death in Leamington*:

> *And Nurse came in with the tea-things*
> *Breast high 'mid the stands and chairs –*
> *But Nurse was alone with her own little soul,*
> *And the things were alone with theirs.*

p.43 *Stanzas: Farewell Life! My senses swim. (Hood's Magazine 1845).* These lines were written when Hood was already near to death and are reputed to be the last he ever wrote.

p.47 *A Parental Ode To My Son. (Blackwood's Magazine 1837 / Comic Annual 1837).* v.2 *Fays* = fairies.

p.49 *Sonnet: The Sweets of Youth. (Comic Annual 1831).* "Elecampane" is a sweet, similar to marzipan, flavoured with extract of leaves and root of the plant of the same name. Thackeray wrote of childhood as *"a rapture of raspberry tarts"* but such sweet experiences for Hood were curbed by ill-health, as he wistfully concludes: *"... that campaign is past".*
l.9 cf. Milton's *L'Allegro* (l.135)

> *Lap me in soft Lydian airs,*
> *Married to immortal Verse,*
> *Such as the meeting soul may pierce*

> In notes with many a winding bout
> Of linkéd sweetness long drawn out.

l.12 *hard bake.* Toffee.

bull's eye. Black and white streaked peppermint sweet.

p.49   *Sonnet: I had a Gig-horse and I called him Pleasure. (Hood's Own 1839).* The pleasures and frolics of a Sunday visit to the country were close to Hood's heart. Possibly an outing to Cobham in Surrey, as Hood had a friend living there and was evidently amused at taking a jaunt up and down Pain's Hill.

l.1   *Gig.* Light two-wheeled, one-horse carriage.

l.6   *Chaise.* Four-wheeled pleasure or travelling carriage, with one or two ponies.

p.51   *Sonnet to Vauxhall. (Hood's Own 1839).* Vauxhall Pleasure Gardens were opened in 1660 and became a model for many such amusement parks all over Europe. They extended from Lambeth to the present site of Waterloo Station. In the great Dr Burney's day, Thomas Arne (the English Scarlatti) was appointed official composer to Vauxhall at a time when the Gardens assumed artistic eminence for their fine concerts and exclusive social gatherings. Hogarth had provided some of the decorations, and the novelists, Fielding, Richardson and Smollett, wrote vividly of the fashionable society parading through the grounds while the orchestra played. At nine o'clock, everyone would rush to see the Cascade and afterwards return to promenade, or take supper in one of the boxes. In April 1749, a rehearsal of Handel's *Music for the Royal Fireworks* attracted a crowd of over twelve thousand people and stopped the traffic over London Bridge for three hours.

The observant "Boz" (Charles Dickens) helps to explain the first line of Hood's sonnet: *"It was rumoured that Vauxhall Gardens by day were the scene of secret and hidden experiments; that there, carvers were exercised in the mystic art of cutting a moderate-sized ham into slices thin enough to pave the whole of the grounds ... We loved to wander among these illuminated groves thinking of the patient and laborious researches which had been carried on there during the day, and witnessing their results in the suppers which were served up beneath the light of lamps, and sound of music at night. The temples and salons and cosmoramas and fountains glittered and sparkled before our eyes; the beauty of the lady singers and elegant deportment of the gentlemen captivated our hearts; a few hundred thousand of additional lamps dazzled our senses; a bowl of reeking punch bewildered our brains, and we were happy."*

l.2 *hark the bell.* A bell was rung to announce the beginning of the firework display.

l.6 *Hengler.* Boz writes of *"the white garments of Madame Somebody (we forget even her name now), who nobly devoted her life to the manufacture of fireworks, had so often been seen fluttering in the wind, as she called up a red, blue, or party-coloured light to illumine her temple"*. Hood had written an ode to Madame Hengler in his first volume of poems *Odes and Addresses to Great People*, where he describes her as:

> *Mistress of Hydropyrics,*
> *Of glittering Pindarics, Sapphics, Lyrics,*
> *Professor of Fiery Necromancy,*
> *Oddly thou charmest the politer sorts*
> *With midnight sports,*
> *Partaking very much of flash and fancy!*

l.7 *Mr and Mrs Pringle.* Possibly Thomas Pringle, the Scottish poet. who died in 1834. He was a friend of Sir Walter Scott and, was secretary to the Anti-Slavery Society in 1827.

l.8 *the Sublime.* Edmund Burke (1729-1797) published *A Philosophical Inquiry into the Sublime and Beautiful* in 1756.

p.51 *Sonnet: The sky is glowing in one ruddy sheet (Hood's Own 1839).* There were many serious fires in London including the Great Tower over the Choir of Westminster Abbey in 1803, a year also when many houses were consumed in Frith Street, Soho. One of the commonest causes of fires were the primitive open-flame footlights in the London theatres, resulting in the loss of the Surrey Theatre (1805), Covent Garden Theatre (1808), Royalty Theatre (1826) and the English Opera House (1830). It was in 1830 that John Braithwaite constructed the first steam fire engine and in 1832, the London Fire Engine Establishment was formed. It was, in effect, an amalgamation of the different companies by Charles Bell Ford, director of the Sun Fire Office. One of the most sensational fires of the period and probably the one Hood has in mind, was the destruction of Drury Lane Theatre in 1809, references to which are also included by Hood in his etching, *The Progress of Cant.* In a letter to his friend Charles Wentworth Dilke, Hood wrote: *"It's an ill fire that bakes nobody's bread, and the Great Conflagration will make an excellent subject"*.

p.52 *A Nocturnal Sketch (Hood's Own 1839).* One of Hood's best known poems in which he takes the ten-syllable line of blank verse, adds an internal rhyme and a cleverly inventive triple-end rhyme. The joke could be said to be carried too far in the last line, where the repeated vowel becomes a monotone which ends in anticlimax. The critic, George Saintsbury, in his essay on the poets writing between 1790 and 1835, says of Hood's "wilder acrobatics" that the line *"Rose knows those bows' woes"* will *"always seem to some respectable people an enormous and disgusting puerility ... Others, who can see in it not, indeed, one of the greatest achievements of human art and genius, but a relishable trifle quite capable of being enjoyed more than once or twice, should let themselves, not in the least pharisaically, say grace before and after it".*

Hood derived great amusement from writing letters to himself as editor of the *Comic Annual: "We can sympathise,"* he says, *"with those admirers of poetry who would wish that* Paradise Lost *had been written in rhyme, whilst others would not have anything else but blank verse. For either of these tastes my discovery will provide, without affronting the palate of any other; for although the lover of rhyme will find in it a prodigality hitherto unknown, the heroic character of blank verse will not suffer in the least."*

l.4 *Drury-Lane Dane.* A topical reference to *Hamlet*, performed by William Macready in 1838.

l.8 *Ducrow.* Andrew Ducrow was born in 1793. Famous and daring circus-rider, the first performer to somersault on the back of a horse.

l.11 *Liston.* John Liston (1776-1846), the first of the comedians to stage his own act as a separate item. He played at the Old Olympic Theatre. His hobby was theology and his humour was of the poker-faced kind. His never-smiling face and his dry wan humour, sent early Victorian audiences into side-splitting laughter.

l.13 *Young.* Edward Young (1683-1765), rector of Welwyn, author of *The Complaint, or Night Thoughts on Life, Death, and Immortality,* a popular poem in its day of some ten thousand lines of blank verse.

l.17 *fobs.* Small pocket in the waistband of trousers or breeches.

l.19/20 *Policeman B.3.* The Metropolitan Police Force was formed by Sir Robert Peel in 1829. Hood probably uses "B" pointedly here, since the blue uniformed corps came to be known as "Bobbies" after their founder. *Charley* = popular name for a nightwatchman.

l.26 *Bulls of Bashan.* Bashan was a small kingdom in the ancient world, famous for its rams and bulls: *"Many bulls have compassed me: strong bulls of Bashan have set me round. They gaped upon me with their mouths, as a ravening and roaring lion."* (Psalm 22 vv 12-13)

l.32 *Reverend Mr Rice*. Headmaster, Christ's Hospital, who officiated at Hood's marriage to Jane Reynolds.

p.53 *No! (Whimsicalities 1844)*

l.7 *Row*. Rotten Row, the equestrian ride in Hyde Park ,London.

l.8 *Crescents*. Part of the new Regency development of central London in the early 19th century, Regents Street being the most famous of the crescents.

l.18 *Ring*. The inner, circular road round Regents Park

p.54 *Domestic Asides, or, Truth in Parenthesis. (Hood's Own 1839)*. In this poem, Hood concerns himself with a small, but by no means insignificant, instance of social insincerity. As with *A Parental Ode to My Son*, Hood draws ironic effects from the discrepancy between what we think and what we say. The poem fits neatly into a whole group of poems which express his life-long hatred of hypocrisy and cant. The elaborate punctuation accentuates the innuendo and emotional inflection.

p.55 *The Doctor. (Comic Annual 1839)*.

v.1 *proctor*. An official in the courts of law.

v.1 *pat*. Exactly suitable.

v.2 *unaisy*. Irish pronunciation of 'uneasy'.

v.2 *Pat*. A typical name for any Irishman.

v.3 *oxalic*. Oxalic acid – a highly poisonous extract of wood-sorrel.

v.5 *flunkey*. A liveried footman.

v.5 *powder monkey*. Boy employed on board ship to carry the gunpowder to the guns.

v.5 *draught*. A dose of liquid medicine.

p.57 *Bailey Ballad: Love with a Witness. (Hood's Own 1839)*. The title, says Hood, originates from the Old Bailey. From his brief, facetious preface to the ballad, we assume that Hood found himself compelled to attend jury service at the Old Bailey, during which time a project came to him of *"a Series of Lays of Larceny, combining Sin and Sentiment in that melodramatic mixture which is so congenial to the cholera morbid sensibility of the present age and stage"*. Young girls employed as domestic servants in middle and upper class houses were vulnerable and frequently the victims of deception.

p.58 *Faithless Sally Brown. (London Magazine 1822 / Whims and Oddities 1st Series 1826)*.

v.2 *press-gang.* Young men were forcibly "pressed" into service in the navy by groups of violent and unscrupulous gangs sent out into the towns by a ship's captain.

v.3 *Boatswain.* Ship's officer in charge of sails and summoning men to duty with a whistle.

v.3 *feint.* A pretence.

v.4 *Swain.* Archaic term for *"lover".*

v.7 *Eye-water.* Tears.

v.8 *Benbow.* Vice-Admiral John Benbow (1653-1702). Commander-in-Chief, Dunkirk 1694, and later in the West Indies 1698-1700. Died of wounds at Port Royal. A naval hero.

v.8 *Gee woe!* Pun on 'gee-whoa!' – an expression used for stopping a horse.

v.9 *Tender-ship.* A tender is a small craft attending a ship to supply provisions and carry dispatches.

v.10 *Fish-woman.* A woman who hawks fish, usually renowned for her flow of invective. A vulgar, scolding female.

v.11 *The virgin and the scales.* Reference to Milton's *Paradise Lost* (Book X, 676): *"By* Leo *and the* Virgin *and the* Scales". Virgo and Libra are signs of the zodiac.

v.15 *eye his pipe.* The pipe was his only consolation.

v.15 *pipe his eye.* Colloquial for "to weep".

v.16 *pigtail.* 17th century name for tobacco twisted into a thin rope ready for chewing. It gave its name to the plait of twisted hair worn by sailors till the early 19th century.

v.17 *berth.* A sailor's sleeping place.

v.17 *The sexton toll'd the bell.* One of the tasks of the sexton in a church was to oversee the funeral arrangements, including tolling the bell.

p.60 *Conveyancing. (Hood's Own 1839).*

v.1 *loco-motion.* Literally, movement from place to place. The word 'locomotive', first coined by William Hedley for his colliery travelling steam engine, was used by Stephenson as the name for the engine on the Stockton-Darlington railway.

v.2 *hacks.* Originally a medium sized horse used for riding. Later the name was applied to a horse let out for hire. Here, the reference is to hackney carriages.

v.2 Jarvis. The name for a hackney coachman, possibly deriving from St. Gervaise, whose symbol in art is a whip.

v.3 Queen Mab. Employed by fairies as midwife to deliver man's brain of dreams. cf. Mercutio's Queen Mab speech in *Romeo and Juliet.* Hood wrote a poem on the theme.

v.3 car. Short for carriage.

v.4 stages. Distances between stopping places for changing and refreshing horses.

v.4 Hatchett's. An important terminus at the corner of Piccadilly and Dover Street, London, for west-bound stage-coaches.

v.4 dickey. Rear seat for servants on a carriage, used when their master drove.

v.5 yard. Inn yard.

v.5 bugle. Sounded to announce arrival and departure. Also used as an advance warning to toll-gate keepers.

v.5 'Ye banks and braes'. From the first line of *Highland Mary* by Robert Burns.

v.6. Gurney. A steam carriage invented in 1829 by Goldsworthy Gurney (1793 -1875), which went from London to Bath and back at a rate of 15 miles an hour.

v.7 Malthus. Thomas Malthus warned that, unless family sizes were limited, population would outrun the food supply.

v.8 conveyance. A triple pun for a carriage, a legal document, and a theft.

p.63 *Sally Simpkin's Lament. (Comic Annual 1834 / Hood's Own 1839).* The poem is subtitled *"John Jones's Kit-Cat-Astrophe"*. *"Kit-cat"* is a small half-length portrait. *"Simkin"* (or *"Simpkin"*) is a foolish person.

p.64 *Youth and Age.* A similar theme is to be found in Lewis Carroll's poem about youth and age, beginning: ' *"You are old, Father William," the young man said'.*

p.67 *Verses Mistaken for an Incendiary. (Comic Annual 1839).* The Swing Riots (1830-1833) in the southern counties of England followed the introduction of the new threshing machines, which were seen as a threat to agricultural employment. Menacing letters were sent to farmers, the machines were wrecked and corn-ricks were set on fire, but the identity of Captain Swing was never established. Social unrest was always feared by those in authority. In this unusual poem, Hood attempts to enter the mind of an anarchic incendiarist (political arsonist), who is prepared to burn everything. In exaggerating the theme, Hood seems to suggest that very little is to be achieved by total anarchy. Hood explores agricultural distress in his poem: *The Lay of the Labourer.*

v.1 *rig.* Practical joke.

v.1 *Sing old Rose, and burn the bellows.* A Cavalier drinking song:

> *Now we're met like jovial fellows,*
> *Let us do as wise men tell us;*
> *Sing old Rose and burn the bellows –*
> *Let us do as wise men tell us.*

v.1 *burn my wig!* Wigs occasionally caught fire on candle flames.

v.2 *snap-dragon.* Another name for flap-dragon: raisins floated in a bowl of spirits and lighted. cf. *Shakespeare's Henry IV: "Drinks of candles' ends for flap-dragons".*

Gallants used to drink to the health of their mistresses with flap-dragon and would frequently have lighted candle-ends floating in the liquor to heighten the effect.

v.3 *up at sixty.* During the 1830s imports of coal to London from Newcastle upon Tyne increased considerably, as did the price to 60 shillings a ton.

v.3 *Old Coke.* Sir Edward Coke (1552-1634) Chief Justice to James I and writer on the law. After his retirement he lived at Stoke Pogis, the setting of Hood's prose piece *The Corresponding Club*, a series of bogus letters concerning *'troubles at Stoke Pogis – treasonable letters – nocturnal assemblages – and conspiracy against an illustrious personage'.*

v.4 *Chabert, the Salamander.* One of the many sensational street performers of Hood's day. A salamander was a mythical lizard-like creature that could survive in fire.

v.5 *burn the old year out, don't ring it.* Echoes of Hood's lines can be heard again in Tennyson's *In Memoriam* in which each line begins with the word *'ring'.* In his poem Tennyson assembles a list of life's negative attributes and seeks to destroy them with life's positives; the incendiarist in Hood's poem seeks to do the opposite.

v.5 *Lang Syne.* In Burn's famous song we find the line: *We twa hae paidl't i' the burn* (i.e. We two have paddled in the stream).

v.6 *Beadle.* Parish official responsible for administering the poor law. On the whole, not a popular figure, as Dickens shows in *Oliver Twist.*

v.7 *postage*. In 1841, Rowland Hill introduced the Penny Postage, using pre-paid adhesive stamps for the first time.

v.8 *rating*. Following the 1835 Municipal Corporations Act, rates to support local services could be levied on all the ratepayers.

v.8 *Paving*. London was paved with flagstones between 1815 and 1825.

v.8 *Burn the gas*. The Gas Light and Coke Company was founded in 1812. Gas-lighting was introduced into London between 1814 and 1820.

v.9 *candles, white or yellow*. Candles were made by melting the harder and less fusible animal fats and had a yellow appearance. Later, candles were made from spermaceti, the white brittle fatty substance contained in solution in the heads of sperm whales.

v.9 *King of all the Greece*. The Greek war of independence from the Turks was brought to a conclusion by Great Britain, Russia and France in the Treaty of London, 1827. Otho of Bavaria became King of Greece in 1835.

v.10 *canters*. Pious hypocrites.

v.10 *Smithfield*. A place outside the City walls where many persons were burned at the stake for their religious beliefs, particularly in the reign of Mary Tudor.

v.10 *Tea-Total*. Richard Turner, a Lancashire artisan, coined the phrase 'Tea-Total' about 1833 when campaigning for total abstinence from alcohol. Some accounts say that he stuttered in pronouncing the word 'total'. His fellow campaigner, the indefatigable Father Mathew, proclaimed in 1838: *"Nothing but te-te-total will do"* when persuading his followers to take the pledge.

v.11 *breeks*. Breeches of clerics.

v.11 *meddling vicars ... Anna's Urns*. The increasing fashion for taking afternoon tea during the reign of Queen Anne occasioned some lines in Pope's *Rape of the Lock* Canto 3. b.7:

> Here, thou, great Anna! Whom three realms obey,
> Dost sometimes counsel take, and sometimes tea.

The Queen was criticised for allowing herself to be influenced by the ambitious Duchess of Marlborough, whose advice on political matters she was wont to accept more readily than that of her own court advisers. The Queen's support for Francis James Edward Stuart, the Old Pretender, was a case in point, which led to criticism from the Bishop of Salisbury, described by the Queen, according to Southey, as a 'meddling parson'.

v.11 *Steers's Opodeldoc*. a special brand of liniment for the treatment of burns.

v.12 *Asphaltum*. The artificial asphalt obtained from gas-works began to be used for pavements about 1838.

v.12 *the Cheapest House in town*. A popular euphemism for the Poor House. The Poor Law had been amended in 1834 and brought about harsher conditions which were vividly portrayed by Dickens in *Oliver Twist*.

v.13 *tales without a head!* Printers frequently placed woodcuts at the beginning or end of a poem or prose piece. These were known as 'head-pieces' and 'tail-pieces'.

v.14 *poor Soup*. Tea-kettle broth, or poor man's tea, was made with hot water, bread, a small lump of butter, pepper and salt. cf. French 'soupe maigre'.

v.15 *Spanish claims*. Rival claimants to Spanish throne had led to periodic foreign intervention since the beginning of the 18th century.

v.16 *that everlasting Poynder*. John Poynder (1779-1849), theological writer. Clerk and solicitor to the Royal Hospitals of Bridewell and Bethlehem (Bedlam). Attacked East India Company for encouraging idolatry. Active in the campaign to abolish suttee, a Hindu practice in which widows sacrificed themselves on the funeral pyre of their husbands.

v.17 *Lucifer*. Lucifer matches came into use about 1834.

v.18 *Parson Stephens's speeches*. Joseph Rayner Stephens (1805-1879), political agitator and charismatic preacher. Chaplain to British Ambassador to Sweden. Wesleyan minister in England (1829-34). Joined the Chartists 1838. Arrested for attending an unlawful meeting at Hyde, Cheshire 1838.

p.69 *Stanzas: With the good of our country*. Hood was never an admirer of party politics. In promoting the "broad flag of England" and unfurling the national banner to proclaim "Britain against all the world", he foreshadows Tennyson's words in *Locksley Hall*:

Far along the world-wide whisper of the south-wind rushing warm,
With the standards of the peoples plunging through the thunder storm;
Till the war-drum throbbed no longer, and the battle-flags were furled
In the Parliament of man, the Federation of the world.

p.73 *The Lady's Dream (Hood's Magazine 1844)*.

p.76 *The Song of the Shirt. (Punch Christmas Number 1843).* Hood's childhood in London made him aware of the destitute humanity which haunted shop doorways after closing time and begged at street corners. As a boy of sixteen in Dundee, he had made friends with a poor journeyman tobacco spinner, whose readings of the Scottish poets Hood affectionately remembered in his *Literary Reminiscences*: *"I still sympathise with the zest with which he dwelt on the pastoral images and dreams so rarely realised, when a chance holiday gave him the fresh-breathing fragrance of the living flower in lieu of the stale odour of the Indian weed: and philosophically I can now understand why poetry, with its lofty aspirations and sublime feelings, seemed to sound so gracefully to the ear from the lips of a 'squire of low degree'. There is something painful and humiliating to humanity in the abjectness of mind, that too often accompanies the sordid conditions of the working classes; whereas it is soothing and consolatory to find the mind of the poor man rising superior to his estate, and compensating by intellectual enjoyment for the physical pains and privation that belong to his humble lot."*

Oliver Elton, in his *Survey of English Literature 1780-1830*, states that the poem *"is in truth an act, a blow, a vindication, a piece of history."* Gilfillan, the Scottish critic, wrote of the considerable impact the poem made on Hood's reputation: *"We blushed when we thought that at that stage of his life he needed such an introduction to the public, and that thousands and tens of thousands were now, for the first time, induced to ask – 'Who's Thomas Hood?' "* The poem was published anonymously at first, and, owing to many false claims to its authorship, Hood was compelled to come into the open after a year, and there is a note of irritation when he writes: *"As I have publicly acknowledged the authorship of the 'Song of the Shirt', I can have no objection to satisfy you privately on the subject. My old friends Bradbury and Evans, the proprietors of* Punch, *could show you the document conclusive on the subject. But I trust my authority will be sufficient, especially as it comes from a man on his death-bed."*

It is ironic that Hood should achieve fame on the publication of a poem which has now lost its initial force since exploitation of labour as expressed in the poem has ceased to exist in this form (at least in law) in civilised, democratic societies.

p.79 *The Bridge of Sighs. (Hood's Magazine 1844). "Of Thomas Hood's four great lyrical poems,"* wrote Mary Russell Mitford in 1852, *"the greatest is* The Bridge of Sighs; *it is one gush of tenderness and charity."* The title of the poem is an ironic use of Byron's *"bridge of sighs"*, which joins the Doge's Palace in Venice to the adjacent prisons. The poem is a fine example of Hood's 'light' treatment of a tragic theme. Waterloo Bridge in Hood's day was the haunt of the despairing poor, bent on suicide. In this remarkable outpouring of compassion for the human condition, Hood succeeded with great skill in drawing together all the threads of his many-sided nature and artistry. It brought him many admirers, not least of whom were Dickens, Browning and Edgar Allan Poe. His greatest admirer in France was Baudelaire, who had read the poem in Poe's lecture on the Poetic Principle. Thackeray, writing of Hood in the *Roundabout Papers*, referred to *"The Battle of Life, in which Hood fell, young still, and covered with glory. The Bridge of Sighs was his Corunna, his Heights of Abraham – sickly, weak, wounded, he fell in the full blaze and fame of that great victory"*. For Browning it was a poem *"alone in its generation."*

p.85 *The Superiority of Machinery. (Whimsicalities 1844 / Hood's Magazine 1844)*. The London Mechanics' Institution was set up in 1823. The spinners of Lancashire went on strike in 1810, the weavers of Leeds in 1834, the potters of Staffordshire in 1835. Strikes in Hood's day were mostly against low wages and poor working conditions imposed by unscrupulous factory owners. Nationally agreed industrial standards were in their infancy and did little to improve the lot of the working man.

p.85 *A Reflection. (Comic Annual 1842)*.

p.85 *On the Arrangement of the Statues in Trafalgar Square. (Hood's Magazine 1844)*. The construction of Trafalgar Square was begun in 1829 and an Act of Parliament was passed in 1844 (the year of Hood's epigram) to secure its preservation. The Nelson Column was completed and the statue set up on the 4th November 1843. The monument towered to a height of 185 feet and was crowned with a colossal statue of Nelson, the victor of the Battle of Trafalgar in 1805. It overlooked Chantrey's equestrian statue of George IV.

p.85 *On a Certain Equestrian Statue. (Hood's Magazine 1844)*. William Jerdan, in his *Autobiography*, records that he attended a dinner given by the Lord Mayor of London for the Duke of Wellington and the committee who superintended the erection of the City equestrian statue near the Mansion House.

p.87 *Party Spirit. (Whimsicalities 1844)*. The loose political groupings of the late 18th century were known as Whigs and Tories. William Pitt, the Younger, had considerable difficulty in forming an administration. Repeatedly defeated in Parliament, he succeeded in keeping public feeling strongly on his side. Charles James Fox (a Whig) unwittingly assisted Pitt by mistakenly adopting tactics to prevent a dissolution. Eventually Pitt's government was strengthened by many leading Whigs and only Fox, with his small party, maintained any effective opposition.

p.87 *On Lieutenant Eyre's Narrative of the Disasters of Cabul. (Whimsicalities 1844).* General Sir Vincent Eyre served in Bengal in 1828 and later as Commissary of Ordnance to the Cabul field force in 1839. He surrendered as hostage to Akbar Khan in 1842 and was rescued by Sir George Pollock in 1843.

p.87 *On the Death of a Giraffe.* The giraffe (or cameleopard), whilst well known to the inhabitants of Africa, was to the early 19th century Londoner a creature of great curiosity. The arrival of one of these animals in London in 1827 caused a great stir of excitement. A present to George IV, it lived only two years, but on the 25th May 1835, a further four giraffes were introduced into the Zoological Gardens in Regent's Park.

p.91 *To Minerva.* Minerva was the Roman goddess of wisdom and patroness of the arts and trades. In Greek mythology she was known as Pallas Athene and her symbol was the owl. Hood refers to himself as Thyrsis, the name traditionally given to the shepherd poet, here working late into the night.

NOTES TO
THE
WOODCUTS

Title Page   *A Great Projector*. The edition of Johnson's *Dictionary* of 1826 defines "projector" as "one who forms schemes or designs" and the verb "to project" has the meaning of "to jut out". Both these definitions are combined by Hood to great comic effect. It is always the third meaning that gives Hood's pun greater focus. In his *Ode to W. Kitchiner M.D.*, Hood refers to the doctor's well-known conversazioni attended by celebrities of the day including Macadam, the poets Samuel Rogers and Thomas Campbell, the abolitionist William Wilberforce, and the Quaker Elizabeth Fry, among others:

> *There came thy Cousin – Cook, good Mrs. Fry –*
> *There Trench, the Thames Projector, first brought on*
> *His sine Quay non –*

The Thames embankment was proposed by Sir Christopher Wren in 1666 and later in the century by William Paterson, founder of the Bank of England. Although the Corporation of London embanked a mile of the Thames in 1767, it was Sir Frederick William Trench (Hood's Great Projector) who initiated the scheme for the completion of the Thames Embankment project.

sine Quay non = sine qua non (i.e. without which something would not be done.)

p.32   *The Lady of "Our Village"*. In 1819, Mary Russell Mitford originally published her series of essays entitled: *Our Village, Sketches of Rural Life, Character, and Scenery* in *The Lady's Magazine*. The essays were published together in five volumes in 1832. Benjamin Robert Haydon's portrait of Mary Russell Mitford was first exhibited at the Society of British Artists in May 1825. The village referred to was Three Mile Cross near Reading:

> *A little world of our own, close packed and insulated like ants in an ant-*
> *hill, or bees in a hive, or sheep in a fold, or nuns in a convent, or sailors*
> *on a ship: where we know every one, are known to every one, interested in*
> *every one, and authorised to hope that every one feels an interest in us.*

Hood's woodcuts illustrate his ability to comment on his subject at a number of different levels. GK Chesterton, in *The Victorian Age in Literature*, singled out this aspect of Hood's genius:

> *The pun is said to be a thing of two meanings; but with Hood there were*
> *three meanings, for there was also the abstract truth which would have*
> *been there with no pun at all.*

There is in addition a "concrete" truth, a topical reference, which had a meaning for the readers of his own time.

p.32 *Fly Fishing.* An illustration to *Letter from an Old Sportsman*, in which Hood describes the comic aspects of the sporting life. He was particularly fond of fishing – Isaak Walton's *Compleat Angler* was a favourite book. Hood imitates the simple fisherman's spelling:

> *In the fishing line I am quite Dead bait, tho I have had manny Good run in my tim, Partickler when the keeper spide me out were I hadent got Leaf. The last tim I went I could hardly un do my rod for roomatiz in my joints, and I got the Lumbago verry bad wen I cum Back, and its atax I doant like. Beside wich I found verry Little big fish on a count of the pochers, who Kil em al in colde blood. I used sumtims to flote and sumtims to fli, but our waters is so over fishd theres no fish to be had, and as I am muscile, I dont like trolling without a catch, the last jack I caut was with my boot, and was only a foot long.*

trolling = to fish with rod and line; also to sing parts of a song in succession
catch = a round, a song performed in parts in succession
jack = a male pike

p.38 *Hook and Eye.* Theodore Edward Hook (1788-1841), a witty writer of light verse, novelist, and successful editor of the Tory paper, *John Bull*. His novels were full of crude fun of the period and, popular as they were, have little interest for us today. He was appointed Accountant General to Mauritius in 1813 but was recalled owing to a £12,000 deficiency in his accounts, or, as he put it, "on account of a disorder in his chest". He was imprisoned in 1823 and his property confiscated. Hook was an amusing dinner companion, as William Jerdan tells us in his autobiography: "Hook, after dinner, gave us two of his usual extemporised songs, one of them characterising all the present company, no one excepted, and few, if any, were spared the satirical lash: so cleverly applied that Captain Harris could not credit that the whole was not preconcerted by Mr Lockhart, Hook, and I!".

The second level meaning is the hook and loop as a dress fastening.

p.39 *Jack of Hearts.* A Jack Tar was a common-or-garden sailor whose hands and clothes were tarred by the ship-tackling. He was seen by many young ladies as a figure of adventure and romance. The theme occurs in the popular comic opera of Hood's day by Charles Dibdin:

> *But the standing toast that pleased the most*
> *Was, "The wind that blows, the ship that goes,*
> *And the lass that loves a sailor!"*

As in *Faithless Sally Brown*, Hood uses the theme a number of times in his poems.

p.40 *Wigwam.* Irish bishops ceased to wear wigs in 1820; bishops in general abandoned them after 1831. This may be the source of Hood's reference.

p.50 *Rocket-Time at Vauxhall – A Prominent Feature.* See note on *Sonnet to Vauxhall* p.51.

p.50 *Fancy Portrait – Madame Hengler.* See note on *Sonnet to Vauxhall* p.51.

p.56 *An Unfortunate Bee-ing.* Spenser, in *The Faerie Queene*, alludes to bees in the Chamber of Fantasy:

> *And all the chamber filled was with flies,*
> *Which buzzed about him …*
> *Like many swarms of bees.*
> *These flies are idle thoughts and fantasies,*
> *Devices, dreams, opinions, schemes unsound.*

Bees are a common symbol in political caricatures, viz. *Blessings of Britain – or – Swarm of Tax Gatherers*, by Williams, in which can be seen large bee-hives (British households) assailed by swarms of drones (tax and rate collectors), and a sturdy John Bull defends his house with a pitch-fork. Hood's woodcuts frequently refer to a topical event. In this case, the reference may be to the publication about 1830 of *The Cottager's Manual for the Management of his Bees* by Robert Huish.

p.78 *A "Constable's Miscellany".* Of all the many compilations of illustrated poetry and prose current in Hood's day, the miscellanies of the publisher, Constable, were among the most popular.

p.86 *Non-Sequitur.* A conclusion that does not follow from what has gone before. An impossible cause and effect are humorously linked together, as in Hood's poem *A Blow-Up*, in which an explosion causes damage and a number of comical accidents follow:

Grave Mr Miles, the meekest of mankind,
Struck all at once, deaf, stupid, dumb, and blind,
Sat in his chaise some moments like a corse,
  Then coming to his mind,
  Was shocked to find,
Only a pair of shafts without a horse.

chaise = a light pleasure carriage
corse = corpse

An amusing example by Dickens of a non-sequitur occurs in the letter from Fanny Squeers to Ralph Nickleby: *"My pa requests me to write to you, the doctors considering it doubtful whether he will ever recover the use of his legs, which prevents his holding a pen."*

End Page. *Ponder's End*. A village near Enfield.

One Sunday morning – (at the day don't fret) –
In riding with a friend to Ponder's End
Outside the stage, we happen'd to command
A certain mansion that we saw To Let .

Hood's *Ode to Rae Wilson Esq*

stage = stage coach

Index of First Lines

Ponder's End

About the Author

Peter Thorogood is a leading authority on the life and work of Thomas Hood. He began his research in 1953 and over the intervening years has assembled a large collection of Hood first editions, autograph letters and manuscripts.

Peter was educated at Brentwood School, Essex, and at the Guildhall of Music and Drama. He proceeded to Trinity College, Dublin where he graduated in 1952 with Honours in Modern Languages, at the same time continuing his studies in piano and composition at the Royal Irish Academy of Music. Since then Peter's professional life has been devoted to teaching, writing and broadcasting. During his time as a lecturer in English Literature and Language with the British Council in London, he was able to make an interesting study of Thomas Hood's work as an etcher and engraver, in particular, Hood's complex caricature *The Progress of Cant*. A further study, *Thomas Hood and his Relations with the Book Trade to 1835*, was published by the Oxford Polytechnic Press.

Peter Thorogood's own published poetry, *Love, Said the Astronomers* (1971), *The Once-Contented Land* (1972), and *Prodigal Son* (1977), were published by Autolycus Press. In 1978 he published a short series of poems *The Suite of Mirrors: Translations and Elaborations from Federico Garcia Lorca*. Like Hood, Peter Thorogood also has a comic side which expressed itself in *A Sent-to-Coventry Carol and Other Verses*. During his time with the British Council he was Radio Talks Critic for the BBC periodical, *The Listener*, and compiled a series on "English Humorous Writing" for the BBC World Service. On being appointed a Senior Lecturer at The Polytechnic of Central London (now the University of Westminster), he was able to pursue his interest in his earlier study on *The Progress of Cant* and its links with the Theatre Royal, Drury Lane.

The period 1985 to 1995 has been largely devoted to the restoration of the medieval house, St. Mary's at Bramber in Sussex, which became Peter Thorogood's home on his taking early retirement. His interest in Hood's life and work, however, has continued: he devised a programme of readings and musical settings of Hood's poetry for the Brighton Festival in 1993 and continues to give occasional lectures. The establishment of the Bramber Press fulfils a long-wished-for ambition to promote a wider interest in the work of Thomas Hood and it is appropriate that *Poems, Comic and Serious* should be its first publication.